The Best of the Human Side

THE BEST OF THE HUMAN SIDE

Managing Our Selves, Our Relationships, and Our Organizations in a Rapidly Changing World

BY LESLIE DASHEW

Beowulf Publishing   Tucson, AZ

Library of Congress Catalog Card Number: 97-94474

ISBN 0-9658028-3-3

Dashew, Leslie 1949-

The Best of the Human Side: Managing Our Selves, Our Relationships, and Our Organizations in a Rapidly Changing World.

First Edition Printing History:
First Printing, September 1997

Printed on acid-free recycled paper.

Beowulf Inc.
6140 East Finisterra Drive
Tucson, AZ 85750

Cover Design by Lisa Malone, Malone & Associates
Book Design by Elyse Dashew, EDX Communications

*For information on how to order additional
copies of this book, contact:*

**Human Side of Enterprise
Suite 700, 210 Interstate North Parkway
Atlanta, GA 30339 U.S.A.
phone (404) 252-7113
fax (404) 255-2906**

TABLE OF CONTENTS

PREFACE

My mission in life is to help people utilize, develop and appreciate their capabilities and those of the people whose lives they touch. On the path to accomplishing this mission, I have had the good fortune to collaborate with many great teachers and guides, clients and family members. This book consolidates in one place many of the lessons I've learned and taught, which I have shared through newsletters, articles, lectures, and seminars.

I would like to acknowledge several people who have helped *The Best of the Human Side* to come to fruition. Elyse Dashew of EDX Communications (my production manager, editor, and niece) was a tremendous resource. Her expertise contributed to the attractiveness, utility, and clarity of this book. Lisa Malone designed the cover to make it beautiful as well as congruent with my love of the Southwest. Amy Tilghman and Jackie Stradley contriuted their editorial talents as well.

The evolution of my ideas and practice as reflected in this book have been greatly influenced by my colleagues in the Aspen Family Business Group: David Bork, Dennis Jaffe, Sam Lane and Joe Paul. I thank them for their inspiration, collaboration and friendship. Mike Cohn, friend and colleague, also contributed to my thinking. My online colleagues, Ken, Jane, Mary, Kathy, also keep me thinking and evolving. Thanks to those mentioned and the many other friends and colleagues who help me continue to learn, grow and write.

PREFACE

Finally, I would like to thank my family, a constant source of inspiration and support: Skip and Linda who write and publish, and share their knowledge generously; Tony, who keeps us aware of the legal issues and helps us maintain our humor; Baleigh, my daughter and greatest teacher; and Kita, who keeps my household running. Last but not least, I thank my dad, Stanley Dashew, whose wisdom has been a constant source of perspective for me. I hope this book serves as inspiration for him to finally document his own life and knowledge.

INTRODUCTION

Our effectiveness starts with our own integrity. For what do we, as individuals, stand? What is our purpose or mission in life? What values guide our actions and use of resources (time, money, relationships, intellect)? And what gives us joy? The clearer we are about who we are, and what we want to do with our lives, the more effective we can be. Otherwise we are reactive to the forces around us.

Therefore the first part of this book includes chapters to help you reflect on your life, purpose and sense of self. Much of this portion was written at the end of the year, as I reflected on the year that had passed and the one about to begin.

At the next level, our effectiveness as humans comes from our ability to relate to others — i.e., interpersonal effectiveness. This includes our ability to communicate, to solve problems, and to work with teams and larger systems such as the complex family business. Thus, Part Two addresses interpersonal skills and team effectiveness.

Part Three focuses on the family business which is a specialty of my practice. The family business is one of the most complex of all human systems, composed of two sub-systems that normally operate more independently. The overlap can cause great confusion when family members/business members are unclear about which "rules" prevail. Even if you are not a part of a family business, I hope you will find insights useful in other complex systems.

All three portions of the book address change. The world is evolving at such a rapid pace that we must be prepared to cope with change and to benefit from it, rather than fall victim to it. Most importantly, we must understand how to make changes in ourselves and to understand our limitations in changing others. This is not an easy process! I have shared some of my own experiences and reflections throughout this book (particularly in the first section) in order to illustrate that work in these areas continues throughout our lives. I have found that when we are courageous enough to share openly, others are more open as well.

PART ONE

INSPIRATION

FOR THE SELF

VISIONS OF SUCCESS:
WINDS OF FATE

One ship drives east
and another drives west
with the selfsame winds that blow.
'Tis the set of the sails
and not the gales
which tells us the way to go.
Like the winds of the sea
are the ways of fate
as we voyage along through life;
'Tis the set of a soul
that decides its goal,
and not the calm or the strife.[1]

Ella Wheeler Wilcox's poem provides a wonderful metaphor for success. It is "the set of the soul" that determines the direction we take, rather than "the calm or the strife." Too often, people blame others, or the economy, or bad luck for their lack of success. Yet those who are truly successful achieve their goals in spite of challenging circumstances.

The single most important factor in high achievement or success is understanding one's personal mission and having a vision of what one wants to accomplish. Further, having a plan of action

---

1. Wilcox, Ella Wheeler. *Winds of Fate.*

to achieve this vision increases the odds of success.[1] The beginning point of personal success is clarity of identity — knowing your purpose, values and goals. This provides your "compass setting" for life. As the winds and currents push you around, you will always get back on course as long as you have clarity in these areas.

3

---

1. See Chapter 3, "Personal Strategic Planning," and Chapter 20, "Finding the Work of Your Life."

2

SERENITY PRAYER:
COPING WITH CHANGE

God grant me the serenity to accept what I cannot change,
the courage to change what I can,
and the wisdom to know the difference.[1]

Such a powerful plea!

One of the themes throughout this book is how we cope with change. This piece describes a relationship to change that helps us realistically assess what we can change and what we must accept. In later chapters, I address tools to help others change. I also discuss coping with the rapid change around us.

Often the end of the year is a time to reflect on the changes we have made, as well as those we have let pass, and to evaluate the wisdom of our choices. As I look back on the past year, I am both awed and humbled by the changes I have experienced and witnessed. I also recognize how easy it is to become complacent and blind, and to stay in a rut.

Accepting What I Cannot Change

I'm reminded once again of my limitations in changing other human beings. I can't. I can only act as a mirror or catalyst for change in another. The older I get, the more I accept this fact and appreciate how hard it is to make significant changes. When I face this reality, I can then choose with what I am willing to live or how to find...

---

1. *Serenity Prayer,* author unknown.

The Courage to Change What I Can

...which is mostly me and my circumstances. Facing honestly and openly who we are, what we are doing and the life we have created is a challenge. The more open I am, the more amazed I am at how blind I used to be. Change requires a huge leap of faith and is most often fostered by the support of our friends. Leaving the security of the known requires a vision of what can be, the confidence to jump over the chasm of fear and....

The Wisdom to Know the Difference

...that this is a change I can create and with which I can live. Once the change is made, it is humbling to truly appreciate both how difficult it is and how small it is compared to the challenges faced by others.

As I struggled with my own fears of change this year, I came across another quote which helped me recognize what I am truly about:

Ships are safe in the harbor.

But that's not what ships are for.[1]

With this in mind, I wish you courage, wisdom, and serenity, and a safe, enlightening voyage.

---

1. Author unknown.

3

PERSONAL STRATEGIC PLANNING

I find the great thing in the world
is not so much where you stand
as where you are moving
to reach the port of success.

You sail sometimes with the wind
and sometimes against the wind,
but you must sail
not drift or lie at anchor.[1]

An issue of great concern to many people is establishing a discipline to help them accomplish personal goals and to make the changes to which I alluded in the previous chapter. These same individuals are often quite successful in helping their organizations set goals and develop plans to achieve them, but they may not apply the same tools to their personal lives. This chapter describes a tool which I call "Personal Strategic Planning" and demonstrates how we can organize ourselves to achieve our own hopes and dreams. Give yourself a full opportunity to complete this plan by allowing several hours of quiet time to consider your true wishes, goals and needs. Although this may take several sessions, complete the plan in as much detail as possible. The greater the specificity, the greater the probability that you will succeed in achieving your goals.

---

1. Holmes, Oliver Wendell.

Lifetime Goals

Write a list of the goals that you would like to complete in your life. Try to be very open to anything that pops into your head. Don't censor your initial thoughts; you can evaluate the list later. Take no more than five minutes to complete this list, and another five minutes to list in priority your top five-to-seven goals. For example:

* Be a good mother

* Travel to Japan

* Sail in Greece

* Write a book

* Have financial security

* Have a fun and challenging career

* Build an adobe home

* Have fun, enriching relationships with many friends and family members

* Mentor young people

* Have a great relationship with a man

* Have a healthy, attractive body

* Have a cactus garden

* Learn more languages

* Help make the world a better place

Three-Year Goals

Now consider your goals for the next three years. List the things you would like to accomplish in that time frame. Again, brainstorm. Don't censor the ideas that come to you. Spend five minutes listing anything you would like to accomplish. Now, prioritize your list so that you have the top five to seven goals for the next three years. You may find it interesting to compare the lifetime goals to your three year goals.

One-Year Plan

The next step is to review the above two lists and develop a list of up to five goals that are the most important to you to accomplish in the next 12 months. Your goals may or may not be consistent with the first two lists. If they are not, consider whether you are heading in the right direction with your 12-month goals or whether you were being completely honest with yourself with the first two lists.

The one-year goals should be written in very concrete, specific terms. For instance, "By the end of this year, I'll lose 25 pounds." Or, "By February of next year, I want to have a clear plan for my career."

The second step in the plan is to take each goal and develop a list of objectives that will help you accomplish the goal. The list should include every objective that must be accomplished — (e.g. "Learn new eating habits by taking a behavior modification class," "Consult a nutritionist to help me develop a weight loss diet that I can follow," "Develop an exercise plan that will help me lose weight and tone up" and several more). The date by which you need to complete the objective in order to reach your goal and deadline should be included as well.

The third step in the plan is to describe those specific action steps required to implement the objectives. In most cases, there will be a series of steps for each objective. List the step, the date by which you will realistically accomplish it and any other person whose assistance you need to achieve the objective, (e.g., "Talk with Dr. Smith to learn about behavior classes and nutritionists, by March 3, 1992." "Schedule a class by April 1, 1992." "Report to Mary which new habits I have adopted by May 1, 1992." etc.).

The plan will take the form of an outline that will follow this format:

- Goal #1
  - Objective #1
    - Action Step #1
    - Action Step #2

Making It Happen

In order for the plan to really be implemented and for your goals to be accomplished, there are several additional steps you may wish to take:

- Review the plan and consider whether it is realistic, given the demands of your life. You may wish to ask someone close to you to review it. Consider the obstacles to each step and make sure you have a strategy to address them.

- Once you are committed to the plan, place the specific action items on your calendar or appointment book to assure that you will have it on your daily agenda.

- Review your progress at least monthly and if needed, revise the dates or steps. You may find that you have left out some steps or have miscalculated how long something might take to achieve. If you review the plan, you can become better equipped at developing effective plans in the future. It is also very encouraging to check off the items you have accomplished. This lets you see your actual progress toward your goals.

There's an old saying: "If you don't know where you are going, any road will get you there!" Nevertheless, if you do wish to accomplish personal goals, planning will increase the odds of success. Each small step accomplished encourages the next. Each goal attained increases our sense of accomplishment and self-esteem.

Inspiration from the
Tao Te Ching

Success is as dangerous as failure.
Hope is as hollow as fear.

What does it mean that success is as dangerous as failure?
Whether you go up the ladder or down it,
your position is shaky.
When you stand with your two feet on the ground,
you will always keep your balance.

What does it mean that hope is as hollow as fear?
Hope and fear are both phantoms that arise from thinking of the self.
When we don't see the self as self, what do we have to fear?

See the world as your self.
Have faith in the way things are.
Love the world as your self;
then you can care for all things.[1]

This is another great challenge of our age: to find balance — balance between our needs and those of others; between work and leisure; between strength and gentleness; between acceptance and the search for improvement. The *Tao Te Ching* provides an ancient source of inspiration as each of us strives for balance in the modern world.

---

1. excerpt from the *Tao Te Ching*

Success always brings new challenges, stretching our capacity to cope. Often, achievement, and the fear of losing it, are accompanied by an absorption in ourselves. The ancient Greeks warned of *hubris,* in which pride and excessive attention to ourselves could be the cause of our downfall.

The *Tao* offers two considerations to address the hazards of success. The first is to set aside our "selves" and focus more on those around us and their care. As we consider the needs of others, our risks and challenges often diminish in scope, as do our fears. When we shift from a focus on our own success to fostering that of others, we solidify our base, which helps us to keep our own balance.

The second suggestion in the *Tao* is to have faith in the way things are, to believe that there is an intended order to the universe. This faith enables us to weather the ups and downs with humility and relative calm.

As I contemplate my own achievements, failures and lessons learned, I continue to gain a deep appreciation of how my clients and colleagues contribute to my growth and success. The more I am able to give to you, the more I receive. However, achieving the balance between giving and receiving is not always easy! Some of us give too much and are uneasy receiving, while others are too quick to take, without thought of sharing. I hope you take time to reflect on your successes and to consider how you can develop balance in your life.

5

WISE WOMEN

In order to thrive in our complex world, we must seek wisdom. As I prepared for a program I presented to women in family business, I was inspired to write the following thoughts. (Note: The barriers which wise women must address are also those faced by men.)

The Wise Woman knows when to offer counsel and when to resist. She understands dilemma and can offer perspective. The Wise Woman has seen enough to appreciate peace; to understand rather than judge.

She is bright, serene, cozy and calm. She has poise, humor and grace. The Wise Woman can tell us what we need to hear to put our minds at ease, but she will also tell us when we are wrong and how to fix the deed. The Wise Woman can be a revolutionary who has vision, passion and drive and won't rest till she makes progress for her cause. The Wise Woman knows when to pick up arms and when to put them down. She can be a courageous lioness defending her cubs as well as a cuddly kitten.

The Wise Woman is a friend who supports us through our greatest trials and cheers us when we triumph; and we know that she values us equally through it all. The Wise Woman takes little for granted. She is not jealous, greedy or possessive; she is patient, persistent and pleasant. She readily forgives herself as well as everyone else, for she knows that neither she nor anyone else can be wise all of the time.

Who is this Wise Woman? Is she our grandmother, our god-mother, our aunt? Is she our mother, our cousin, our friend? Is she our daughter, our niece or our nanny? Is she our sister, our sister-in-law or step-sister? Is she our employee, our boss or our colleague? Is she our nurse, our doctor or our preacher?

She is the woman who is there for us at just the moment we need her; with the right word or touch or look. And she is there within us all, just waiting to come out; waiting for us to tap the eternal wisdom we have gained over the ages. Ready to be of assistance. Ready to act. Ready to be.

Come, let us find our Wise Woman within and share her with ourselves and with each other. Let us overcome the barriers to finding her. Liberate her from self doubt or compulsiveness, from resentment, hurt and fear. Free her from isolation, shyness and pain. Let her come into the light and shine her radiance on us all.

Welcome, Wise Women!

Five New Lessons About Change

My own process of learning and evolving is reflected in my news-letters. The following chapter represents some of my recent thinking about change. It also summarizes many of the themes captured in earlier chapters of Part One — topics such as graceful anticipation and incorporation of change; faith and trust in inherent order; and clarity of identity and purpose.

Capitalizing on Change

In the last year, I have been looking at how we can organize human systems in a way that takes advantage of the tides or the currents rather than trying to swim against them. How can we incorporate the inevitable changes in the world in our organizational lives and make them advantageous to us? What I am presenting to you is the essence — the principles of what it takes to capitalize on change — rather than the details of a "change management program." These principles are at the heart of elaborate programs and books on re-engineernig, employee empowerment, self-managed teams, and Total Quality Management. I will share with you some of my current thoughts about how we manage ourselves, our relationships and our organizations in this world of rapid change. I say "current" in that my thinking is evolving as I learn from the new sciences and other cultures around the world.

Lesson One: No Permanence

I don't expect permanence of ideas or stability of processes. I expect, even relish change....I don't expect myself to have THE answers, since the questions keep changing. In fact we even have to change our thinking about change!

The prevailing paradigm is that "people don't like change." Allow me to challenge that paradigm:

- How many of you like to have just routine — doing the same thing over and over again?

- How many of you like to find new ways of doing things that make life easier, more efficient and more profitable?

Since many people indicate that they don't like to be stuck in a routine and that they do like to find new ways of doing things, we find that we don't all resist or dislike change. We typically resist change when we don't understand it, or when we don't see how it will benefit us.

Life is about change. Our bodies are continuously changing. New cells are growing and old ones are being constantly discarded. The speed of change in the world around us is accelerating and if we maintain the old mindset that we don't like change or that people resist change, we will find ourselves swimming against the tide. We can reduce stress and frustration by acknowledging that life is change, so we may as well work with it. We must keep alert and vigilant for both the new questions as well as solutions that work. If we expect evolution, we create the mindset, the attitudes, and the work environment to take advantage of it.

Lesson Two: Self-Organizing Systems

Some of my friends and family members might tell you that I am "controlling." On the Myers-Briggs Type Indicator[1], I am a "J" by nature (preferring judgment to perception) which means I like to

---

1. See Chapter 10, "Type and Teamwork," for more information on the Myers-Briggs Type Indicator.

have a plan and work my plan. I don't like to leave much to chance — I would rather make things happen. Underlying that old behavior is a lack of trust that things happen naturally or that systems are inherently orderly. Sometimes I fear that life is chaotic.

What I have come to appreciate from the study of new sciences such as chaos theory is that life is self-organizing. There is order in what appears to be chaos, but we have to step back and look at it from sufficient distance and time. Margaret Wheatley, in a seminar on self-organizing systems, described the termites she observed in South Africa. These termites create complex twenty-to-thirty-foot-tall structures out of dirt. In order to create these structures, the termites have to maintain close to l00% humidity at all times (in dry South Africa!) and keep the temperature at seventy degrees. They do this by digging deeper to access moisture at the appropriate times. The termites have no leaders. They wonder around, bump into each other, notice what needs to be done and do it. For example, they build well-balanced bridges. When a group starts on one side, another group notices, and starts on the other side. Without the assistance of engineering, supervision or computers, they meet in the middle, constructing a stable, strong bridge: In other words, they act as a self-organizing community.

The older I get, the more I trust that there is order in the universe and that, if I keep myself from getting too anxious, I will be able to see the order or patterns. Often, our anxiety about lack of control or order makes it difficult for us to see clearly or to solve problems effectively. At those times, we try to force a predetermined outcome rather than allow it simply to evolve. Life has the capacity to organize itself and doesn't always need us to do it.

Lesson Three:
Identity, Relationships and Information

While I am "getting out of my own way," how do I help other people to organize, to get work done effectively and efficiently?

Whether I am helping a client system or organizing a team of my own, this is another challenge to address.

Lesson Three, then, is to help people find clarity of identity and purpose; to create access to the relationships or people and to the information that they need.

I start most of my consultations by asking people about the purpose or mission of their organization. Or, with family business situations, what is their vision for the future? What do they want to accomplish as a family at this point in history? With that purpose clearly articulated, all stakeholders can focus their attention on accomplishing it. The clearer we are about our purpose, the greater the odds are that we will achieve it.

This applies to teams, families and organizations as well. When a group of people are focused on a shared mission or vision, they can mobilize their creative energies to make it happen. This also assumes that they have access to the resources and information that they need. An example of this occurred at Southwestern Bell.

The entire management team of Southwestern Bell was out of town attending a meeting, when a major natural disaster occurred. The staff that remained there quickly mobilized themselves, organized a plan and effectively met the challenge, assuring that the utilities returned to operation in an efficient manner. This was accomplished without a designated leader: another good example of self-organizing systems. Afterwards they took the opportunity to explore why we all seem to be at our best during the worst times. Their report suggested:

* There was an instant sense of teams and purpose, a sense of connectedness.

* No time wasted on the trivial.

* No heroes: everyone a contributor.

- No manuals.

- You work with whatever is available (tinker/make do).

- Jobs are new, different, strange, yet people also play in their own position.

- Communication is wide open.

- Leaders emerge.

- Formal leaders play subordinate roles more readily.

- There's no risk--it's already a disaster.

First and foremost, the Southwestern Bell employees had a clear, shared purpose. Second, they were able to access the people and information they needed without any "hierarchies or politics" to interfere. And third, the mission was compelling to them. If it is important to them, people will organize themselves to get the job done. They will keep trying to solve the problem. A clear mission gives meaning to work. People want meaningful work.

Lesson Four:
Interdependence Is Necessary for Survival

When we are clear about our shared objective and that we need each other to achieve it, we recognize our interdependence. Lesson four is about recognizing our interdependence: acknowledging that we can't do it alone. Many of us grew up believing we had to be strong and independent. Independence is a myth. It is much like looking at a grove of aspen trees. On the surface, the aspens appear to be a large group of separate trees. Under the surface, one can see that they are really all parts of one system. Each aspen tree grows from the root of another which then pushes up through the earth giving the appearance of a separate, new growth.

On the surface (especially when we are young) we may appear independent. As we mature, we recognize that we are not independent, not separate. What we do effects everyone else in our system. The more we acknowledge the interdependence, the more we pay attention to the relationships, and to communication. As we take care of these relationships, we increase our effectiveness through the channel of collaboration. Our effectiveness in relationships becomes even more critical as we face an increasingly complex world, with information multiplying faster than ever and change occurring at a faster rate.

Lesson Five: Know Thyself

This leads to the final point: Know Thyself.

In order to lead, manage, be part of a team or any relationship, and to adapt to changing conditions, we must be clear about ourselves.

What is our personal mission in life? What is most important to us? What are our values? Without clarity in this area, we cannot build personal integrity. It is also important that we know ourselves in terms of skills, knowledge and resources. With our recognition that we cannot do it alone, we need to look to others who have complementary talents with whom to be partners.

Knowing our own assets and limitations allows us to look at changing opportunities and determine what we can handle and what we cannot. Further, we must be aware of the mindset we bring into each situation, for our assumptions about the situation create our reactions to them. Our attitudes impact our effectiveness in more ways than anything else. We are all familiar with the concept of a self-fulfilling prophecy: if I doubt that I can do something, I will prove myself right! Seeking out and changing our self-defeating mindsets, prejudices and habits are important aspects of knowing ourselves.

Application To Business

Now, how does this apply to running a business? One of the biggest challenges most managers have in running a business is the management of human resources. How do we get people to do what we want them to do with enthusiasm, creativity, accuracy and a collaborative attitude? Most of us try to push and pull people to do that. The point here is that with the rapidity of change, with the differing attitudes of various employees and with the lack of the old employee-employer contract about long-term commitment, the old push/pull doesn't work. We have to engage employees in our quest, help them to find meaning in the work, give them the opportunity to organize and to collaborate with us as we scan the environment for change, new opportunities and challenges. For many of us, this requires a shift in our attitudes. We must fine-tune our skills and be willing to change the nature of our working relationships. We will need all of the resources around us for that challenge.

You may find the following *Native American Grace* useful as you face change in the future:

> *O Great Spirit*
> *whose voice I hear in the winds*
> *and whose breath gives life to all the world,*
> *Hear me!*
> *I need your strength and wisdom.*
> *Let me walk in beauty and make my eyes ever behold*
> *the red and purple sunset.*
> *Make my hands respect the things you have made*
> *and my ears sharp to hear your voice.*
> *Make me wise so that I may understand*
> *the things you have taught my people.*
> *Let me learn the lessons you have hidden in every leaf and rock.*
> *I seek strength,*
> *not to be greater than my Brother,*
> *but to fight my greatest enemy —*
> *myself.*[1]

---

1. Author unknown.

PART TWO

HUMAN

EFFECTIVENESS

So What You Are Saying Is:
A Guide to Successful Listening

Our effectiveness in all relationships depends upon our ability to communicate. Yet one of the most frequent issues in marriages, parent-child relationships, partnerships, schools, and businesses is the "failure to communicate." When this phrase is heard, it most often refers to the reason for a mistake or the feeling that one has not been understood. In twenty-five years of working with people in all kinds of settings, I have found that the most common reason for this failure is the lack of well-developed listening skills. This chapter describes strategies to improve your listening abilities and demonstrate your understanding of what has been said.

How do you know if someone has really heard you? When someone says "I understand," what is it that he or she understood?

Have you ever wondered why voices get louder and louder and points-of-view get restated over and over again in a heated discussion?

Do you ever get frustrated when someone seems to be on a different wave-length, or maybe takes off on a totally different tangent in a discussion that is important to you?

The challenges described above are common to most of us. Effective communication or having confidence that your message was received as intended is a rare experience. Instead, most of us get frustrated, angry or (worse) repetitious when we find that people are not listening or "hearing" us.

Why Is It So Hard?

The process of listening is very challenging and the odds are against our understanding one another unless we really work at it. A number of barriers interfere with understanding, three of which are listed below:

❧ Assuming you know the rest of the story.

A very common listening error is to hear the first part of the statement and assume you know the rest. Rather than patiently hearing the whole story, we interrupt and interject our own perspective prematurely. Sometimes we do know what someone is going to say, but often we miss an important point, in addition to rudely indicating that our perspective is more important than theirs.

❧ Words are symbols.

Words are symbols for images, ideas or objects and our use of words may conjure up a picture in the listener's mind that is different from what the speaker has in mind. Consider the simple example of ordering a steak cooked "medium-rare." In some restaurants, meat cooked medium-rare looks as if it was just cut off the cow, while at others, it has a gray-brown coloring with no signs of pink. We attribute different meanings to words. Often, we falsely assume that others hold the same meaning as we do, and this, too, contributes to misunderstanding.

❧ Internal and external distractions.

We are all susceptible to distractions while listening, such as noises or activity in our immediate environment. I describe these as "external" distractions since they occur outside of us. Internal distractions can be just as disruptive to the listening process. These distractions include growling stomachs, emotional reactions to the speaker or his words, or going off in our own heads. We start thinking about something sparked by the speaker, and this causes us to lose track of his words. In either case, distractions often contribute to our missing important aspects of a speaker's message and can leave us with a false or incomplete understanding.

A key element of most miscommunication is our assumption that we fully and accurately understand the speaker. With all the inevitable barriers to communication, this is rarely a safe assumption.

The single most effective tool to enhance listening and understanding skills is to confirm your understanding with a reflective response.

Paraphrasing: Reflecting Your Understanding

If you practice the following listening rule, your listening ability will improve 100%:

Leslie's Golden Rule: After hearing someone complete a statement, reflect back to your understanding of the message to confirm that you have accurately heard the speaker before adding your perspective or response.

Paraphrasing — the most common reflective response — simply means re-stating another's message in your own words. When you paraphrase, you:

* Let that individual know that you are interested in accurately understanding her perspective, thereby demonstrating your interest and concern for her.

* Verify that your understanding is correct, or have the opportunity to revise it if you have misunderstood.

* Let the person know that her message has been received, so that she no longer needs to press her perspective and, typically, will be more open to listening to yours. You reduce defensiveness and build trust.

* Demonstrate your understanding, rather than claiming it.

Typical paraphrases begin in the following way:

25

* "So what you are saying is..."

* "If I understand you correctly...."

* "In other words...."

* "To summarize, then...."

* "Let me check out my understanding..."

Or, you may give an example that illustrates the speaker's point (called "advancing a tentative example"). For instance, "Would a pin-striped suit without cuffs be the type of apparel you are recommending?" If the speaker responds with "Exactly!," you know that you have heard/understood correctly.

When you paraphrase, in essence you are testing yourself. Most of us pay closer attention to a teacher's words when we know that we are going to be tested. Thus, if you commit yourself to "Leslie's Rule" and practice regular reflective responses, you will find that you are paying closer attention to the speaker — as if you were expecting to take a test. You will also find that this practice increases your ability to overcome distractions, to determine what meaning the speaker attributes to her words, and to refrain from interrupting.

Paraphrasing is important even when you think the statement you have heard is simple or straightforward. Your judgment may be based on a misunderstanding. Even if you think you're "going overboard" with paraphrasing, you probably aren't doing it as often as needed. As hundreds of participants in my Listening Skills Workshops have experienced, paraphrasing increases effectiveness, efficiency and relationships both on and off the job.

"So, Leslie, what you are saying is that we should paraphrase whenever we listen to anyone."

"EXACTLY!"

8

DIALOGUE

Listen...
I do not know if you have ever examined how you listen,
it doesn't matter to what
whether to a bird,
to the wind in the leaves,
to the rushing waters,
or how you listen in a dialogue with yourself...
If we try to listen we find it extraordinarily difficult,
because we are always projecting our opinions and ideas,
our prejudices, our background, our inclinations, our impulses;
when they dominate we hardly listen to what is being said.
In that state there is no value at all.
One listens and therefore one learns,
only in a state of attention, a state of silence
in which this whole background is in abeyance, is quiet;
then, it seems to me
it is possible to communicate.[1]

I have found that one of the most prevailing concerns about communication is how to constructively resolve conflict. Most people will tell you that they hate conflict; many of us avoid it. Yet conflict is merely a difference of opinion. There are few relationships without differences. Thus our ability to understand these differences and how they are formed is key to our ability to have healthy relationships. The art of dialogue is one of the most useful practices I have found to help us understand the nature of our differences and a practical approach to resolving them.

---

1. Krishnamurti. *Talks and Dialogues.*

In my most recent efforts to gain new understandings of teamwork and organizational effectiveness, I have been studying the concept and methodology of "dialogue." This chapter shares some preliminary thoughts with you. Personally, I am striving to create opportunities for true dialogue; and professionally I hope to assist my clients in their ability to establish dialogue in their organizations.

"Given the nature of global and institutional problems, thinking alone at whatever level of leadership is no longer adequate. The problems are too complex, the interdependencies too intricate, and the consequences of isolation and fragmentation too devastating. Human beings everywhere are being forced to develop their capacity to think together — to develop collaborative thought and coordinated action."[1]

As Isaacs points out, the increasing complexity of the world means that we are becoming more dependent upon each other to address or solve problems. Our capacity to join forces and come up with synergistic approaches will perhaps be the most important factor for success — or even survival. To me, the heart of this is the ability to be truly "on the same wavelength" with others who offer a variety of perspectives, experiences and attitudes. We need to communicate in such a way as to establish genuine openness, real understanding and shared assumptions. In other words, to have a dialogue.

The Greek roots of "dialogue," *dia* and *logos*, connote "meaning flowing through." So a true dialogue is a form of communication that yields a shared meaning. As we communicate our own

---

1. Isaacs, William N. "Taking Flight: Dialogue, Collective Thinking, and Organizational Learning." *Organizational Dynamics.* Autumn 1993.

perspectives and, more specifically, our own assumptions, we create a pool of shared information. For example, imagine a circle of people looking at an octagonal container in the middle of the circle. The octagon is fully perceived only as each member of a dialogue shares his/her view of the container. Since each sees only one or two sides of the container, it is not fully comprehended until all of their views are collected. Once all the views are shared, a common picture is formed of the container and the meaning can be understood.

I am reminded of the Indian story about the 6 blind men touching an elephant. Each feels a different part of the elephant and describe the elephant from their own point of view: "The elephant is flat and thin and has stiff little hairs on one side," said the blind man touching the elephant's ear.

"No," argued another blind man, who was feeling the elephant's leg, "the elephant is tall and cylindrical and I can almost get my arms around him, like a moving tree trunk," and so on. Each man had an incomplete and erroneous picture of the elephant. If they had collected their observations, their experience and the assumptions underlying their conclusions, they might have come up with a shared and more complete view of the elephant.

"Listening with my heart I find meaning.

For just as the eye perceives light and the ear sound,

the heart is the organ for meaning."[1]

The process of dialogue requires that we listen with our hearts as well as with our ears and heads. We must be open to differing perspectives, rather than judgmental. The more certain I am,

---

1. Brother David Steindl-Rast.

the more difficult it is to explore meaning. Dialogue can only occur in a safe environment where people feel comfortable questioning their own conclusions, exploring their own assumptions and openly listening to potentially diametrically differing views. The challenge for most of us is to allow multiple points of view to be held in the conversation and still stay connected: living with paradox.

The process of dialogue starts within ourselves. In order to be open to develop shared assumptions, we must be aware of the assumptions underlying our own conclusions. Thus the first step is to uncover our own assumptions. This is generally referred to as "listening to the listener," understanding our own mental models and/or determining the steps we took to come to a conclusion. The second step is to question the assumption and allow that it may not be valid. My assumption is that, in order to effect a dialogue, I must stay in a position of inquiring, rather than knowing.

I wrote the following poem to help me to remember this goal:

Stillness in me.

Hard to capture.

Breath-ful

quiets the chatter.

Sharing what comes through that breath

is what's important.

It's new; it's me.

It's focused

where it should be.

Sharing our own assumptions, then, becomes the next step in creating the dialogue. Much like a stew we might cook together in the kitchen, we have placed the onions in the pot and now await someone else to add the meat. With each assumption placed in the "pot" we come close to understanding what might be the complete picture or "stew." As long as we don't feel that our assumptions are ourselves (i.e. that we do not become overly attached to them and thereby defensive), we may shift our perspective and arrive at shared assumptions. Like the stew which is more than and very different from the individual ingredients, our shared assumptions can become a new view that may be a novel solution and/or a basis for shared commitment and action.

"Dialogue's purpose is to create a setting where conscious collective mindfulness can be maintained."[1]

Although it may seem patently obvious that having a dialogue would be advantageous, it is important to understand its potential. As people learn to communicate in this manner, the quality of the conversation improves, creative solutions arise and commitment to common plans increases the probability of successful action.

My interest in dialogue arises from my work with highly conflicted situations in business teams, family businesses, etc. I have found that people can become motivated to resolve conflicts if I help them to determine a common mission and to understand that they are interdependent. If we move into a safe environment where people can reflect on and question the assumptions upon which they have based conclusions about one another, then openness and conflict resolution can occur. My own experience has been mirrored by those doing more extensive work with dialogue. For instance, seemingly intractable labor-management disputes have been resolved through a dialogue process. Major progress in

1. Isaacs, William N. *ibid.*

addressing a community's health delivery problems has occurred through the dialogue process. In Colorado, a community pooled the perspectives of hospital administrators, community activists, consumers, and county health officers to begin exploring their assumptions about healthcare delivery. The dialogue process allowed them to let go of traditional adversarial positions and find a shared set of assumptions which guided further planning and improvements. It is possible to move quickly to a sense of community utilizing the dialogue process.

My sense of dialogue as an emerging communication technology suggests that it may be a very subtle and powerful tool through which we can foster understanding, harmony and creativity. It certainly warrants more study and, well, dialogue![1]

---

1. For more information on dialogue, see:
Bohm, David. *On Dialogue.* Ojai, Ca: David Bohm Seminars. 1990.
Schein, Edgar. "On Dialogue, Culture and Organizational Learning." *Organizational Dynamics.* Autumn 1993.

9

CAN WE TALK?

The following chapter illustrates the practice of dialogue with a concrete example of a situation and a tool to use in addressing conflict.

As the world becomes increasingly complex, we seem to be getting worse at some basic skills — most notably, communication. In order to adapt and survive, we need to use dialogue to explore a variety of perspectives and achieve real understanding among our colleagues, employees, suppliers, customers, and family members. Yet just when it is becoming even more crucial to develop sound communication skills, people often tend to argue instead.

When people argue, it is usually over their conflicting conclusions. As long as we focus on conclusions, our horns will stay locked. We can try to untangle our horns by exploring the assumptions beneath our conclusions. This enables us to identify the core of our misunderstanding or difference and address differences in a more constructive manner.

People often perceive things differently. Our perceptions (part fact, part emotion and part subjective personal beliefs) feed our assumptions. When assumptions are based more on emotion and personal beliefs and less on facts, they may not be accurate. The best way to test the validity of each person's assumptions is to articulate them. The diagram on the next page illustrates how this process works.

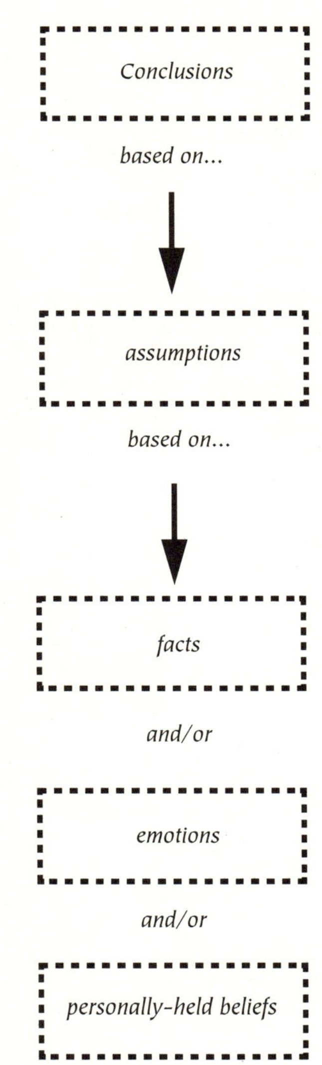

Before you voice your opinion, consider your underlying assumptions and where they come from: Do you have adequate facts? Are they based on emotions or "irrational" beliefs? Should you ask more questions before you draw a conclusion?

Following is an example of how family business members used this process to resolve escalating conflicts. One son of a business founder was resentful that he wasn't allowed to join the family business. This set off a series of conflicts within the family. We started by looking at the son's conclusion that he should have a job in the business - we wrote that in the top box. We asked him to name the assumptions on which he based his conclusion, and wrote his answer - that all family members should have a role in the business - in the second box. Next, we asked him for data he had to support his assumption. First, he mentioned that his cousin was given a position when he was the son's age and second, that he assumed that's why they had the family business in the first place.

This information gave us an opportunity to understand the origin of the son's feelings and to explore a solution. The father was able to explain that the cousin came in to the family business because the company was very short-handed at that

35

point and that the cousin had some experience that was relevant to the business. Dad admitted he thought it would be nice if the business could provide opportunities for the family, but he never made a statement to the family that this was a given. The reality is that he has to base hiring decisions on the purpose of the business, how it makes money and who can add value, rather than on entitlement. We were able to help the son see that as a future owner (based on his father's estate plan), it would be more appropriate to hire people with experience to help build the business and that the son's payoff would be as an owner, not as an employee. He was able to see that guaranteeing everyone a position in the company would undermine the effectiveness of the business.[1]

1. This chapter was originally written for the Cohn Financial Group Newsletter, *Transitions and Traditions*. March 1995. Volume 4, Issue 2.

10

TYPE AND TEAMWORK:
IT TAKES ALL TYPES TO MAKE A TEAM

Our ability to communicate is enhanced when we understand our different styles of communication. These styles — or preferences — are best described by the Myers-Briggs Type Indicator. The Myers-Briggs Type Indicator (MBTI) is one of the most useful tools in helping us appreciate, rather than be frustrated by, differences in communication, organization of our lives, our sources of energy and our outlook on life. The following chapter describes the MBTI in its application to effective teamwork.

In the early days of space exploration, pioneers in the aerospace field pulled together experts from many different fields to solve the complex problems of how to explore the vast unknown worlds in the sky. A group of aerospace engineers couldn't figure out on their own how to send rockets and people into space: a wider range of knowledge and approaches was needed. They called upon physicists, architects, engineers, psychologists, astronomers and many other specialists to collaborate. Yet each of these professions had its own paradigms, philosophy, methodology and jargon. A great challenge was to get people with such diverse perspectives to communicate on the same wavelength. In meeting this challenge, the field of "team building" was born.

In the more than forty years since the field began, we have refined our understanding of the processes of building teams, but the essential challenge remains: how to capitalize on the diversity of perspectives represented in healthy teams. Having homogeneous teams fosters a quick sense of mutual understanding and ease of communication. However, it also yields incomplete understanding of situations and shallow, even flawed solutions. In the last ten years, we have come to more fully appreciate the strength that comes from broad-based input to teamwork and the commitment that accompanies involvement in consensus decision-making.

39

The variety existing in teams today is more often one of values, thinking styles and personalities, rather than professional disciplines (although that exists, too). Thus, managing diversity today means understanding the mindset of other team members — the way they think, organize themselves and communicate.

Contributions of Different Types

Carl Jung, the grandfather of Type Psychology, believed that our thinking processes can be divided into two categories: (1) how we perceive or obtain information and (2) how we process or make decisions about that information. He observed that we gather information through our five senses and through our intuition. We come to conclusions based on two types of criteria: logical, rational "thinking," and a more personal, subjective "feeling" approach.

We use all four of these approaches, but have a preference for one way of gathering information and one way of coming to conclusions. People who prefer to gather information via their senses pay close attention to information they can touch, hear, see or smell. They like facts and concrete realities and are interested in immediate experience. Action is what drives them. People who prefer intuition need to find associations or connections among things, and are interested in possibilities. They operate more on hunch than on concrete facts. Meaning is what drives intuitives. People who prefer to come to conclusions based on more logical, rational bases, or "thinking types," tend to want structure in their lives; on the other hand, "feeling types" or those who make decisions based more on human values and what will preserve harmony are motivated by caring.

Each of us also has a dominant preference among the four types (sensing or "S", intuition or "N", thinking or "T", and feeling or "F") — we have one cognitive or mental process that primarily guides us. We see evidence of this dominant preference when we look at what activities are most important to us as team members. Intuitives, as noted above, are driven by meaning and will be most concerned about the mission of the team: why we are gathered together, and where we are headed. Dominant thinking types seek organization: they will look at how we are structured to achieve our mission, and focus on the goals and objectives of the team. Team members with a dominant preference for sensing are action-oriented; they will seek the specific action steps designed to achieve

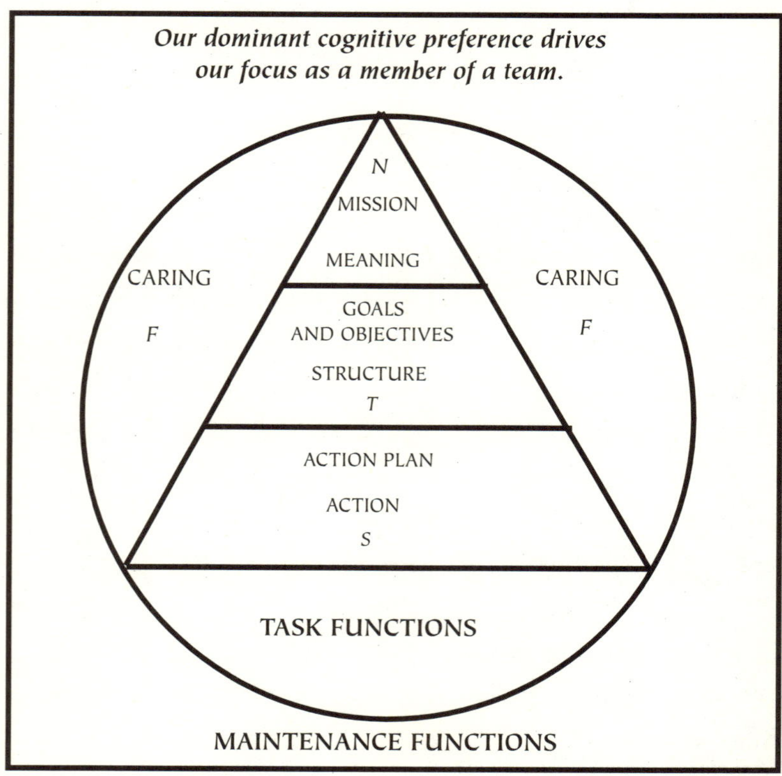

the team's objectives. All three of these team members are primarily concerned with the tasks of the team. Feeling types are more concerned with the process of the team or how the team works together to get the job done. They are focused upon the caring for or nurturing of team members.

All four team functions are needed. If a team has members representing the different profiles, automatically there are forces in place to address the needed tasks. If not, team members must consciously work to address the area that might otherwise be neglected. For instance, in many large businesses there is a preponderance of thinking and sensing types and a lack of feeling types. Thus, the process of working together as a team may be neglected and mutual support is often missing. Entrepreneurial organizations are often lead by dominant intuitive types who will look at creative visions but lack the structure and attention to day-to-day details to actualize their dreams. If the complementary types are not empowered members of the team, lack of a full range of perspectives may keep the organization from success.

Isabel Briggs Myers (co-author of the Myers-Briggs Type Indicator, the personality profile tool used to determine preference) noted the following: "The clearest vision of the future comes from an intuitive, the most practical realism from a sensing type, the most incisive analysis from a thinking type and the most skillful handling of people from a feeling type. Success for any enterprise demands a variety of types, each in the right place. Opposite types can supplement each other in any joint undertaking. When two people approach a problem from opposite sides, each sees things not visible to the other."

Attitudes

In addition to explaining our cognitive functions, type psychology also describes our attitudes toward the world around us and our preferred approach to organizing our lives. These preferences also impact the way we function in teams. The first dimension describes the focus of our attention: upon the world inside of ourselves ("Introversion") or the world around us ("Extraversion"). People who prefer introversion draw their energy from within themselves, are most interested in concepts and ideas and tend to study problems in depth. Individuals who prefer extraversion are more focused on the world around them, obtain their energy from interaction with others, and solve problems by "thinking out loud." They are concerned with action and take a broad view on issues. Introverts provide depth to the team, while extraverts provide breadth. The thoughtful approach of introverts can easily be lost in teams dominated by action-oriented extraverts. Thus, careful attention to inclusion of all members in team discussion will help to capitalize on the quieter members' insight. Allowing introverts to think about any issue before it is discussed will encourage their participation. Giving extraverts a chance to talk it out before coming to a conclusion will assure that you have heard their best ideas.

The last dimension refers to how we organize our activities in the world. Some people prefer to live planned, organized lives; getting things completed gives them joy. These "judging" types assure that a team has a plan for getting the job done and will push for decisions to get made. "Perceiving" types, on the other hand, prefer to have flexibility and spontaneity in their lives and to look at and understand options, rather than decide upon one. Perceiving types help teams adapt and respond quickly to change.

Utilizing "Type" in Teams

Understanding type psychology helps team members work well together in several ways. First, when we understand the basis of our differing perspectives, we can be more understanding and less judgmental. For example, I may misinterpret the reluctance of a member to participate and share his perspectives as indifference or arrogance if I didn't understand that he is an introvert. As an introvert, he may not participate because he: (a) hasn't seen an opening in the discussion; and/or (b) hasn't thought about the issue in sufficient depth to feel comfortable giving an opinion. A sensing type might grow impatient with an intuitive's drive for clarity about vision while the thinking type feels undue pressure by the feeling type to focus on harmony in the group, rather than on the task at hand. Knowing our own and others' preference allows us to appreciate the perspectives of others and to address differences in a more objective, rather than aggressive manner. We often find ourselves working with people who are very different in nature from ourselves. Knowledge of type helps us overcome the barriers of differences to enable us to get our job done, particularly when we can more readily communicate on each other's wavelength.

Second, understanding type can help in planning a project and selecting the members of the team. Ideally, the composition of the team should include individuals with the needed knowledge and skills and the type make-up to foster teamwork. Recent research has documented the assumption that teams are most effective when they are composed of heterogeneous types. I have had clients report to me that project teams have been twice as efficient when composed with a mixture of type in mind. In addition, there are occasions when the task requirements of the team might dictate the selection of types. For instance, a project that requires careful attention to detail and in-depth thoroughness might call for more introverted sensing types on the team. Knowing what drives each member of the team can also help us to select the most appropriate person for assignments on the team.

As Henry Ford once said, "Coming together is a beginning; keeping together is progress; working together is success." Our ability to work together is largely a function of our ability to capitalize upon our diversity and not allow our differences to divide us. Tools such as the Myers-Briggs Type Indicator and knowledge of type psychology can greatly aid us in coming together as a team, understanding what each of us can contribute to the team and fostering the attainment of our goals.

11

Myers-Briggs Type Indicator:

A Personal Perspective

The Myers-Briggs Type Indicator (MBTI), which has been available to psychologists for more than thirty years, is based upon Carl Jung's typology of personalities. The MBTI provides information on four dimensions of personality or preferences:

Extroversion - Introversion

Sensing - Intuition

Thinking - Feeling

Judging - Perception

The forced choice test yields sixteen possible combinations of these four dimensions which tell you a great deal about yourself. For example, I took this test twenty years ago and then again recently. My type, both times, was ENTJ. A quick rundown on me would include that I am:

- Extroverted — at ease with the environment

- Intuitive — aware of possibilities, insightful, use ingenuity

- Thinking — logical, decisive, demanding of efficiency, and

- Judging — organizationally oriented.

Those of you who know me well can evaluate how accurately that brief description applies to me!

(Note: The Myers-Brigg Type Indicator must be administered and scored professionally.)

We have found that instruments like the MBTI help us understand strengths and areas needing development. They help to explain how we see and experience the world. They provide a clear picture of how we differ from others so that we can better comprehend the variety of reactions and choices others make. These tools can provide insight into what types of occupations would be most congruent with our approach to life.

12

PLEASE UNDERSTAND ME

In all of my consultations, I seek to understand others and to help my clients to work and live with others in greater harmony. I have found the MBTI to be a great tool for fostering understanding. The following quote from a book on Type Psychology[1] captures the hope I hear from many clients for the understanding and acceptance of our individuality.

"If I do not want what you want, please try not to tell me that my want is wrong.

Or if I believe other than you, at least pause before you correct my view.

Or if my emotion is less than yours, or more, given the same circumstances, try not to ask me to feel more strongly or weakly.

Or yet if I act, or fail to act, in the manner of your design for action, let me be.

I do not, for the moment at least, ask you to understand me.

That will come only when you are willing to give up changing me into a copy of you. I may be your spouse, your parent, your offspring, your friend, or your colleague. If you will allow me any of my own wants, or emotions, or beliefs, or actions, then you open yourself, so that some day these ways of mine might not seem so wrong, and might finally appear to you as right for me. To put up with me is the first step to under-

---

1. Kiersey, David and Marilyn Bates. *Please Understand Me: Character and Temperament Types.* Del Mar, CA: Prometheus Nemesis Book Co. 1984.

standing me. Not that you embrace my ways as right for you, but that you are no longer irritated or disappointed with me for my seeming waywardness. And in understanding me you might come to prize my differences from you, and, far from seeking to change me, preserve and even nurture those differences."

To illustrate the challenge we have in accepting others' differences, consider your own reactions:

You easily converse with other people, bringing up your own point of view, "thinking out loud." Do you ever get frustrated when someone important to you is less communicative, or seems to think a long time before sharing a point of view?

Or, you like to think about something for awhile before you open your mouth. Do you look down upon people who "put their mouths in gear before their brains" and speak without thinking?

You like to plan ahead and make arrangements. Do you ever get upset when your partner wants to "hang loose" and wait to see what he feels like doing later?

Or, you like to be spontaneous and you get irritated when your partner wants to "box you in" by making plans well in advance. You can't understand why your colleague Is always looking at the obstacles to a new idea; why can't he just try it?

Or, your colleague is never satisfied with what is; he's always trying to change things.

These are examples of how our own preferences color what we expect of others, as well as how they impact our reactions.

13

Building the Right Team

Working effectively as a team requires work! Clarity of purpose or identity and recognition of our interdependence are only the beginning. Teams require other maintenance tasks, too, such as clarifying work guidelines, plans and mutual expectations. Thus it is important to pay attention to the right teams and make the appropriate investment. The following chapter will help you do just that.

The Paradox

Managers today must contend with an important paradox in productivity: (1) good team work is an important vehicle to enhance productivity and organizational effectiveness; and (2) building teams takes time, which is a scarce commodity. Thus, it is essential that managers carefully select which groups of people are truly teams and have the potential for synergy. These teams, then, provide the greatest payoff for your investment.

The Team

Three criteria have to be met for a group to be defined as a team:

❦ Members must have a clearly defined common mission or goal...

❦ Which can only be achieved through the collective efforts of members (interdependence) and...

❧ They recognize this interdependence.

Katzenback & Smith[1] captured these criteria in their definition of a team: *"A team is a small number of people with complementary skills who are committed to a common purpose, set of performance goals, and approach for which they hold themselves mutually accountable."*

The concept of mutual accountability for a common goal resulting from combined work efforts is at the heart of the definition of "team." By contrast, a working "group" may have the same or similar goals, along with common interests, and can even benefit from sharing mutual support and learning, and yet still not have the interdependence of a team. In the latter case, efforts to build teamwork may be useful, but not the highest priority.

Making the Best Investment in Team Building

The highest-performing teams require an investment in their teamwork process. Thus (1) selecting teams and (2) selecting the right teams in which to invest your time, attention and at times, outside assistance, is important. The "right" team is that team whose outcomes are critical to the company's success, either by virtue of its role (e.g., a true leadership team), timing (e.g., their outcome and effectiveness is particularly important to the company at this time or by a certain deadline) and/or position in the company (e.g., many other individual or collective efforts depend upon this team).

Fostering high performance teams includes these steps:

❧ Be very clear about the team's charter and the significance of their output to the organization.

---

1. Katzenback, Jon R. and Douglas K. Smith. "Wisdom of Teams." *Harvard Business Review.* March/April 1993. p. 112.

❧ Allocate time for members to create the appropriate team processes, structure and climate as well as task accomplishment. Successful and productive teams invest time in building trust, understanding and familiarity via informal as well as task-related activities.

❧ Collectively translate the charter into specific, attainable goals, a clear picture of the skills and knowledge needed and then the roles that each member will play in order to accomplish the mission to which they have committed. Further, high performance teams consider what factors are essential to their success (i.e., critical success factors) and translate those into a set of agreements or ground rules for this operation as a team. (see notes to add ground rules)

❧ Review team progress on tasks. Where are we in terms of our initial plans? Do we need to adjust our timeframe or directions in order to process how are we doing as a team? Are we meeting our commitments to each other? Are we stepping on anyone's toes? Are we capitalizing on our potential for synergy? High-performing teams are clear about their outcomes and are flexible and responsive to changes and opportunities that may impact them.

❧ Recognize and celebrate short-term and overall successes. Ongoing motivation and commitment are enhanced by reminders of one's achievement and how it contributes to the organization's well-being.

Teaching or Fishing for Success?

An old parable suggests: "If you give a man a fish, he'll eat for a day. If you teach him how to fish, he'll eat for a lifetime." In our task-oriented, short-term focused culture, it is often hard to take the time to teach and develop our people. Each team that learns how to work effectively together carries both that knowledge and the resulting success with them to the next project or work team. The investment pays off in multiples as the team culture takes hold in the organization and employees recognize the importance of their individual contributions, their impact on the effectiveness of others and, when collective goals warrant conscious, dedicated teamwork.

51

14

FURTHER THOUGHTS ON TEAMWORK

The following chapter offers some ideas for assessing your own teams.

Is Your Team Synergistic?

Synergism is defined as "cooperative action of discrete agencies such that the total effect is greater than the sum of the two effects taken independently." When $2 + 2 = 5$, you have synergy. A group of people can either function like ten individuals, each "doing her own thing," or as a cohesive team lending their talents toward the group's goals. Studies have documented that a well developed team yields innovative, productive solutions much more often than when team members feel that meetings are a waste of time, that they must watch what they say, or when they feel that "The boss will decide anyway, why say anything?!"

Team building is a process of consciously looking at how well a group is working together: whether talents are being fully utilized, morale and commitment are high, problems are readily identified and resolved or where communication is cautious, members feel unappreciated or underutilized, and/or power plays are the focus of attention. Team building can most readily occur with expert facilitation to help identify barriers to effective teamwork and to put into place strategies to foster synergy and thus more productive use of team members' energies.

The difficult decision for most team managers is how to determine if they NEED team building. Consider the following questions:

❧ Do you leave team meetings with confidence that much has been accomplished and that your team will follow through as planned?

❧ Do you feel all members actively participate and openly share their perspectives and opinions?

❧ Are team members comfortable giving each other direct feedback and confronting problems within the team?

❧ Are you and other team members energized and positive after team meetings; feeling good about the team and the meeting?

If you answered "no" to any of these sample questions, you are underutilizing your staff, and the potential for increased productivity is untapped. It is time to consider developing this resource through team building!

Sources of Teamwork

If you are not part of the solution, you are part of the problem!

Sometime ago, I provided consultation to a small organization undergoing major change. Morale was low, turnover was high, employees did not trust management, or even each other at times. In short, the climate was quite negative.

Then a major change occurred and the suspected "source" of the problems was gone. The problems, however, did not disappear; many took time to remedy. Removing the target for the stones did not remove the stones. The personnel who remained were still ready to blame others. By doing so, they became a major source of problems.

Teamwork depends upon good leadership and good membership. Team members who look to their leaders for all the answers are abdicating their rights and responsibilities. Some suggestions for good team membership:

❧ Don't assume the leader sees all and hears all; do share your observations and concerns;

❧ Don't gripe about each other behind the scenes; do discuss it openly if you feel others are not carrying their share of the load;

❧ Don't just point to the problems; do try to suggest possible solutions;

❧ Do put yourself in each others' shoes; try to be understanding and supportive;

❧ Do set team goals and review how well you are doing as a team.

The sources of good teamwork are all of the members of the team. A team cannot be effective without the commitment of its members to the team, its goals and its progress.

15

Confrontation!

One of the greatest challenges to our relationships with others — personally and professionally — is dealing with conflict or confronting others.[1] As members or leaders of teams, we often must confront behavior, attitudes or work performance that is counter-productive. A technique that is quite useful is behavior feedback, which is described below.

Tips on Confronting: Consider Your Purpose

Is your purpose to vent your anger and frustration or to help the individual to grow and "do it better" next time? If it is the former, STOP. This is not the setting to ventilate. If it is the latter, present your feedback to the individual with that stated purpose. Confrontation can then be productive for both of you.

Wear Their Shoes

Try to understand the other person's point of view. What purpose did the behavior serve? Was it a misunderstanding on his part? Ask for his thinking about the issue before you confront: that will prepare you to present your request in a manner conducive to change.

---

1. See also Chapter 9, "Can We Talk."

Be Specific

Describe the behavior that is a problem specifically; don't assume that the individual knows what he has done to create a problem for you. Then describe how or why the behavior is a problem for you. (That same behavior may not be a problem for them or others.)

Suggest Options

Give corrective suggestions and/or alert him to what you need to do if the problem persists. Options are often better "digested" than threats or commands.

Be Assertive

Don't be passive and let others walk all over you. At the same time, don't resort to aggressive behavior (yelling, screaming, threatening, beating). State your understanding of their behavior or position, indicate your concern or problem with the situation and suggest alternatives that would meet your needs. That's being assertive!

Guidelines for Giving Behavior Feedback

* *Never describe characteristics of people; only define their behavior, as specifically as possible.*

* *Use behavior feedback as soon as possible after the behavior has occurred.*

* *Use behavior feedback the first time behavior occurs — it is less effective with habitual behavior.*

* *When you state your emotional feelings, have the courage to reveal your real feelings — and avoid commonplace words like "angry" or "frustrated."*

* *This technique can and should be used for behavior that is pleasing to you as well as for behavior that is displeasing.*

FOUR-STEP METHOD FOR GIVING BEHAVIOR FEEDBACK

Describe what the person is doing:	Describe the concrete or observable effect on you:	How does it make you feel:	What you want to happen or what you will do:
When you play your stereo loudly at 3:00 a.m.,	the neighbors call me to complain,	and I feel really annoyed.	Please confine your use of your stereo to reasonable hours.
When you ask me to complete a report at 4:30 p.m., when I typically leave at 5:00 p.m.,	it requires me to be late to pick up my daughter,	and I feel conflicted and worried.	I would like you to try to get work to me earlier.
When you are in 45 minutes late for your shift,	I have to keep the previous shift longer, and they are tired,	I worry about them and I am concerned about your commitment.	You need to make a habit of being on time or I may have to recommend your termination.
When you clean up the house as well as you did yesterday,	I don't have to rush home to take care of it.	I feel very appreciative.	I hope you will continue to be so helpful.

PART THREE

Family Business Effectiveness

16

Substance Abuse in the Workplace

A common dilemma for many people is how to confront chemical dependency or other compulsive disorders. This can be particularly difficult in the workplace. This chapter offers guidance on how to cope with the challenge.

The statistics are staggering: one of every three families is facing substance abuse in the immediate family; businesses are facing a $136 billion loss in productivity due to alcoholism alone; and drug use adds to that tab. Absenteeism, sickness, accidents, worker's compensation claims and medical insurance costs are additional expenses to companies as a result of alcohol and drug use. So prevalent is this problem that it has become a major campaign issue in the presidential elections. Campaign promises in 1988 resulted in legislation requiring drug testing and a drug-free workplace in transportation jobs and other sensitive positions in American industry. In many ways, businesses have struggled for years and will continue to struggle with drugs in the workplace. This epidemic requires supervisors and managers in all businesses to be prepared to deal with substance abuse and dependency on the job. The following guidelines provide some measures supervisory personnel can take to help address this challenge.

Be Clear About Your Role

Remember that your job is to supervise employees in the performance of tasks that accomplish the company's goals. Thus, you must confront employees who are not performing up to standards and coach them on job skills or knowledge. You are NOT a therapist trained to identify and treat emotional or chemical dependency problems. If an employee's personal problems are interfering with work performance, it is time to call in help.

Know Company Policies, Procedures and Benefits

Your first line of assistance comes from company policies on performance deterioration. Consult your human resource contact or your supervisor to clarify the policy on warnings, company-supported assessments (e.g., use of an employee assistance program, or E.A.P.) and the specific procedures for doing so. It is also important to be familiar with company insurance benefits. Do they cover inpatient/outpatient treatment for emotional and/or chemical dependency treatment? Once you are prepared with this information, you can confront the employee in a supportive way by saying something like "You seem to be having some problems that are interfering with your work performance (give examples). I am not qualified to say what is causing these work problems, so I would like to encourage you to get some outside help. The company will support your getting help in the following ways (e.g., pay for treatment, leave with pay, etc.). We need you working at your best and we are concerned about you."

Communicate Clear and Specific Job Descriptions and Standards and How Their Performance Compares

In order for you to discuss job performance deterioration, you must be clear about performance expectations. Thus, be prepared with job descriptions and performance standards with which employees are familiar. When you review performance (at least twice each year under normal conditions), it is important to document the level at which the employee is functioning. If the employee begins to demonstrate poor performance, you can then point to his/her performance records over time. It is important to carefully record the ways in which the employee's performance has declined (e.g., increased absenteeism, decreased productivity, attitude changes, etc.) with numbers and specific examples. Employees who are chemically dependent will typically deny they have a problem unless you confront them with indisputable evidence. Again, your job is to assure that job tasks are completed appropriately and in a timely manner. It is your responsibility to confront any employee who does not carry his/her load. Confrontation can be the most constructive gesture that the alcoholic or addict ever receives, as it may lead him/her to recovery. Stick to a discussion of behavior on the job.

Recognize Patterns of Performance Deterioration

The chemically dependent employee will progressively deteriorate in her capacity to handle the job:

* Absenteeism and tardiness increase with improbable excuses.

* Problems with concentration and confusion yield lower productivity, higher error rate, poor judgment and lowered efficiency.

* Work performance may be spasmodic, with periods of high then low effort, time spent intensely working or absent from one's post.

* The employee comes to work or back from breaks in obviously mood-affected conditions (giddy, "speeding," blurred speech or vision, excessively irritable or "paranoid").

* Relations with customers or other employees deteriorate because of over-reaction to real or imagined criticism, irritability, or tenseness.

* There is evidence of mood and attitude swings.

* He borrows money from co-workers, holds resentments, etc.

If patterns of such behavior appear, it is reason to refer for assessment. Many of the behaviors may occur for other reasons, so don't assume chemical dependence is the only cause.

Understand the Nature of Chemical Dependency

The drug- or alcohol-dependent person uses her substance COMPULSIVELY and rigidly denies that she has a problem. Compulsivity is defined as the irrational, illogical, irresponsible continued use of drugs/alcohol despite adverse consequences. This type of use is often evidenced by the way the drug or alcohol is used:

* Lying about how much, when and where it is used (minimizing).

* Guarding the supply (assuring that it will be available whenever and wherever).

* Thinking about and using the substances inappropriately (as the center of one's life).

* Taking alcohol or non-prescribed drugs as "self-prescribed" medication (to sleep, calm nerves or stop "the shakes").

* Taking the drug to prevent anxiety, pain, depression or other discomfort.

* Driving, appearing in public or telephoning in altered states of consciousness.

* Trying to "cure" oneself by changing brands or places the substance is used.

❧ Continuing to use despite warnings by people she loves and respects.

Chemical dependency is a disease that requires treatment to overcome. An employee who is given the option to get help and return to a productive work life OR leave the company has a greater chance to obtain the needed help than one who is simply fired or allowed to continue to work in an incapacitated fashion. The supervisor who is prepared to constructively confront such an employee provides a great service to the employee and the company.

17

Assumptions About the Future

As if all that is not enough to cope with, another challenge facing us is the rapidity of change. The following chapter describes my assumptions about the future and some related strategies to develop.

In 1995, I was asked to speak at the Annual Meeting of the World Future Society. The topic was "Investing in the Future: The Personal, Corporate and Societal Balance Sheet." Rather than imply that I somehow knew what would happen in the future, I shared my assumptions about the future based upon observations from my work with many client organizations.

Fluid Organizations

Organizations will be much more fluid than in the past, changing their shapes, sizes and processes with greater ease. They will use individuals or sub-contractors more and more as strategic directions require, and for defined periods of time. No longer will people expect to work for organizations for a life time...or even for a major portion of their careers.

Leaders as Conductors

A leader of an organization in the future will have to be much like the conductor of an orchestra: she will need to select the music to be played, be able to hear it (internally and vividly), select the right instruments and musicians to play it, help them understand her vision and pull them together to make beautiful music to match or exceed the quality she had envisioned. The skills of that leader will include many of the same we need now, but a new emphasis will be upon tapping external resources that may not have experience and facilitating the joint effort of the "ensemble." Like musical performances, the next project may utilize some of the same players, but not necessarily.

Autonomous Individuals Aligning for a Goal

Individuals and small assemblages of people will pull together with each other or with larger organizations to achieve specific, time-limited goals...aligning strategically and letting go. Individuals will be more self-contained, working out of their homes, airplanes, boats and/or cars, connecting electronically and by satellite.

Continual Change Requires the Ability to Reshuffle

One of the keys to success in the future will be our ability to pinpoint the specific talents, skills, aptitudes, personality preferences and interests of each individual. This way the individual can "shuffle" these resources in a multitude of configurations in order to offer flexible ways of contributing in a satisfying manner. He will be better able to meet the continually changing needs of clients or employers.

We used to know the rules of the game, as well as what cards it would take to win. For instance, in gin rummy, players would hope for a run of seven in a row of the same suit; or three of one and four of another. As we move into the future, we find that the rules of the game are continually changing; we no longer know what combinations will help us. So the guiding strategy will be to know what cards you have in your hand and which are your favorite or "strongest suit," and to scan the environment to see what game is being played and what rules are in place. Then you can assemble your hand accordingly.

In addition, you may be playing with changing partners, and it's important to know your own strong suits as well as theirs.

Trump Cards: Interpersonal And Intrapersonal Skills

I would speculate that the "wild card" that can be played in any game will be interpersonal and intrapersonal skills. Interpersonal skills include the ability to:

- Dialogue (raise awareness of our own individual assumptions and develop shared assumptions with others).

- Create a container for dialogue.

- Seek and give feedback.

- Establish rapport and trust quickly.

- Exchange information and perspectives using good verbal skills.

- Scan the environment to readily identify opportunities, resources, supports and/or affiliations.

- Clarify and negotiate boundaries.

- Disengage constructively.

Intrapersonal skills include understanding your:

- Personality preferences (e.g., through personality inventories such as the Myers-Briggs Type Indicator).

- Skills.

- Talents.

- Knowledge.

- Needs for affiliation versus privacy.

- Attitudes of openness or acceptance of change.

- Willingness to learn.

All these attributes will be critical to success in this new world.

Back to the Community for Affiliation

Individuals will address their needs for affiliation via communities centered around residences, spiritual or religious beliefs, recreational interests and/or intellectual and skill areas.

Because of our changing work affiliations, other sources of stability may become more important. We may chose to belong to social, professional or religious groups which will become our primary referent group.

We might find that our home is again a major focal point (look at the explosion in the home-improvement fields). With more people working at home, this will undoubtedly continue to be a greater focal point. It may mean that the pendulum will swing back towards more emphasis on the stability of family life, or perhaps we'll move towards more communal living situations, with a sense of community and continuity.

The desire for communities based on similar values and connectedness may give rise to new business institutions with multi-faceted missions. For example, Ben and Jerry's mission is to sell ice cream as well as incorporate a recognition of their interdependence with employees, their community and the planet.

Individual, Organizational and Societal Progression: Dependent ➤ Independent ➤ Interdependent

Systems (individuals, organizations, societies) go through an evolution from dependent to independent to interdependent. As we move toward interdependent, we pay closer attention to the connection between the sub-systems.

Individuals have traditionally been more dependent upon their employers. Many are now becoming independent and working on their own. Soon they recognize their interdependence and work at collaboration/partnership. Similarly, businesses have been dependent upon the worker. Now, feeling independent for economic reasons, many are downsizing and are using people more as contractors, sub-contractors or partners. Their attention will become focused on these relationships when they recognize that they are not independent, but interdependent. Similarly, as a society, we were initially dependent upon the earth. We later came to believe we were independent of it. We are now beginning to recognize our interdependence and are taking better care of the earth. As organizations foster that recognition, they attend to their responsibility to the earth, as well.

Requirements for Good Partnerships:

Success in affiliations depends upon individual and organizational ability to "partner," once we recognize our interdependence.   I have some observations on what makes good partnerships:

* Shared values: shared vision at the top, mutual respect, common cultures (such as common beliefs about process improvements).

* Common goals: agreed upon strategies, sharing of risks and rewards, openness to expand common horizons.

* Collaborative attitudes: willingness to trust, sharing of information; commitment to work on the relationship, conflict resolution strategy and sense of fairness/win-win, persistence in ironing out the differences between organizations and they way they operate, flexibility to allow the relationship to evolve.

* Clear boundaries: written agreements, guidelines and processes; clear roles, responsibilities, authority, accountabilities; focus on and appreciation of complementarity of the parties (including differences); areas of cooperation and areas of competition clearly stated.

❧ High-level communication abilities: ability to dialogue or to truly understand each other and establish a shared mental model (which allows us to cross over those cultural barriers that exist between organizations or parts of organizations); willingness to communicate openly and regularly; and ability to address differences.

David Whyte in *The Heart Aroused*[1] shared his observations about the future:

"The twenty-first century will be anything but business as usual. Institutions must now balance the need to make a living with a natural ability to change. They must also honor the souls of the individuals who work for them and the great soul of the natural world from which they take their resources....preservation of the soul means the preservation at work of humanity and sanity...Above all, preserving the soul means preserving a desire to live a life a man or woman can truly call their own."

---

1. Whyte, David. *The Heart Aroused.* New York: Currency/Doubleday Publishers. 1994.

18

REFLECTIONS ON COPING WITH CHAOS

Following are some additional thoughts on coping with the future, the apparent chaos and inherent order.

For the last 20 years we have become acutely aware of the impact of rapid change on the world and ourselves. The rate of change continues to accelerate and increasingly, people talk about how difficult it is to cope with the unabated change. Yet there does not seem to be a slowdown in our futures. In fact, leaders of organizations all around us are instigating more and more change within their institutions in order to respond to new opportunities and to avoid decline, decay and obsolescence. "Continuous improvement," "reengineering" and "reinventing" organizations have become approaches (and buzz words) used throughout business, health care and even government to enhance effectiveness and value. These are some of the tools used at the organizational system level to manage in a rapidly changing and increasingly competitive world.

In fact, organizational consultants have begun looking at new models of the world to help clients understand how to cope with change. Some have turned to the science of physics to find answers and are looking at chaos theory. There are lessons we can learn from chaos theory which will help as we move quickly into the 21st century. For instance:

❀ Chaos theory suggests that even in times or circumstances that appear to be totally chaotic, patterns exist which can be discerned, if we look long enough and stand far enough away. In other words, things may not be as confusing as we think, given some objectivity.

❀ "Chaologists" point to the incredible interdependence of the earth. What we do on one part of the planet may impact another part without our knowledge or intention. This is referred to as the "butterfly theory": a butterfly flapping its wings in Buenos Aries can impact the weather system in Chicago.

❀ Chaos makes it difficult for us to control circumstances, but we can identify principles inherent in the patterns, allowing us to work with the trend, even if we can't change it.

The dilemma with which many people are coping is how to adapt to the changing conditions while maintaining one's own integrity. "Do I become a chameleon and change my color continually in order to survive?" "Do I dig in my heals and just do it the same old way, since next month a new process will arise anyway?" I believe a balance must be achieved between preserving our integrity (that is, our core values, our approaches that have been consistently effective and our own sense of personal mission) with being flexible enough to develop with the times. The anthropologist Angeles Arrien[1] describes a Native American belief system called the "Four-Fold Way" which contains much wisdom for our times. The Four-Fold Way includes four guidelines: show up, pay attention, tell the truth without blame or judgment and be open (not attached) to the outcome. To build on the Four-Fold Way, I have elaborated the following:

---

1. Arrien, Angeles. *The Four-Fold Way: Walking the Paths of the Warrior, Teacher, Healer, and Visionary.* New York: Harper Collins. 1993.

❧ Show up.

We cannot cope with chaos by withdrawing, or we will drown. We must come to the table, adding our unique perspectives to provide the objectivity or data needed by someone else at that moment in time.

❧ Pay attention.

Identifying the patterns in chaos requires careful attention, as does understanding our actual and potential impact on the world. Paying attention also helps us to identify what is working (and what is not) so that we can develop the best approaches to take us forward. (Note: Most of the process improvement/total quality programs involve close attention to how things are done, and to quantifying results.)

❧ Tell the truth without blame or judgment.

By sharing our observations without judgment, we can look for opportunities to continue what works and let go of what doesn't without fostering defensiveness. Creating a "learning environment" implies that we can safely offer what we know and what we don't know without fear of blame or judgment.

❧ Be open (not attached) to outcomes.

Since chaos makes it difficult to control, trying to achieve a specific outcome and time frame may not always be possible and often leads to frustration and discouragement. This does not mean we stop striving, but we must be flexible and ready to consider a range of outcomes that are more workable in the newest situation.

Remember two reassuring thoughts also shared by chaologists and by me: (1) we, as living systems, come equipped with the capacity to change, and change we will to survive; and (2) order is inherent in the universe. Given the opportunity, we will evolve towards and find greater and greater degrees of order...despite the appearance of chaos!

19

BUSINESS FAMILIES:
THE CHALLENGE OF FAMILIES WHO WORK TOGETHER

This portion of the book is derived from a collection of articles I have written over the past 15 years regarding life in the family business. As a collection, they provide substantial insight into the challenges faced by family businesses. Here you will find concrete strategies to address these challenges, to capitalize on the opportunities inherent in an enterprise built by kin who share a business venture.

This chapter offers a general overview of the situations faced by family businesses.

When you think about family businesses, what comes to mind? The Ewing Brothers from the soap opera *Dallas*, with their jealousy, greed and back-stabbing? Or real-life family empires like the Bingham newspaper family, torn apart by infighting? Or the neighborhood ethnic restaurant you frequent where the parents, grandparents and children all work together to cook, serve and clean in a joyous, harmonious fashion?

Whatever image comes to mind, family-owned businesses are a phenomenon to which more and more of us are paying attention. Family-owned businesses are increasing in size and impact at a never-before seen rate as many couples and families are starting businesses together. There was an 82 percent increase from 1980 to 1985 in the number of businesses started by couples (265,398 to 482,993). And there is a strong trend for women to start their own businesses, especially when they reach the "glass ceiling" in large corporations. Women-owned businesses have increased in numbers from two-and-a-half million in 1980 to over four million in 1986: an increase of over 63 percent (close to twice the increase in businesses owned by men). In addition, since many new businesses were formed at the end of WWII, these family businesses are now facing the crisis of succession, another reason for new attention to family businesses.

When we define "Family Business" as one in which family members have legal control, 90 percent of all U.S. businesses are family businesses. They produce one-half of the gross national product and employ one-half of the country's workforce. Of these businesses, many employ multiple family members. It is to these families that our attention is directed in this chapter.

Creating or Solving Problems?

Family business may be the answer to some dilemmas in our modern lives, but they can create many others. For example, many women begin their own businesses when they find that they can no longer progress in the large American corporation. Having one's own business can yield flexibility in child care arrangements — another challenge of our modern times. Contrary to past generations when working for a large corporation meant long-term employment security, many employees feel insecure working for these firms during this era of hostile corporate takeovers. Many people feel that if they have their own firm, they can be sure they will be able to take care of their own.

Families who own businesses bring special advantages to the business. Typically, families whose names are attached to a business have a greater commitment to the business success, have a longer-range perspective (generations vs. current quarter) and often create a caring environment for employees. The advantages to a family in business together include the opportunity for jobs for family members, revenue for them, flexibility in roles and policies and more control over one's destiny. Many entrepreneurs tire of the limits on their creative and earning potential while working for others. Finally, many families find that sharing a business experience gives them "something in common" to discuss and brings them closer together.

Yet working side by side with members of one's family can be very stressful, resulting in problems both in the family and in the business. We often see inter-generational disputes, role conflicts, communication problems, rivalry with the business and an assortment of family problems played out in the business arena.

One example of inter-generational conflict is the 60-year-old father who can't let go of his control of the business while his 35-year-old son wants to make his mark through the creation of new products and new business strategies. The father wants to maintain status quo; he's tired after 40 years of running the business. Yet his identity is tied to the business and, like many entrepreneurs, he doesn't know what he would do or even who he would be without the business.

Another common problem is role conflict: allowing family members to join the business because of (or making decisions on the basis of) their importance in the family, not because of their value to the business. These roles often collide. Consider the daughter who takes care of everyone at home and is loved for that, yet at work is not a good supervisor because she has trouble holding employees accountable for their work assignments. Many mothers and fathers find themselves in a bind when they see that having their child in the business is a mistake. As a parent, they find it difficult if not impossible to fire their child; as a boss they realize it is a poor business practice to keep an incompetent employee on the job. Stew Leonard, of Connecticut supermarket fame, relates such a story. He invited one "problem employee" son to his house for a swim and said, "Son, being in a family business can be very tough. I have to wear so many hats. I'm putting on my boss' hat now: you're fired! Now I'm putting on my father's hat: Son, I heard you lost your job. I'm sorry. What can I do to help?"

Communication problems in the family may also end up interfering with sound business practices, yielding frustration and costly errors all around. Conflicts between the family and the business for shared resources such as time and money also surface as issues in family-owned businesses. Many sons and daughters in family businesses have felt "sibling rivalry" with their parents' firm: "Sometimes I feel mom and dad eat, drink and sleep 'hardware!' They almost never have time to take us anywhere. I sometimes feel like the business is more important to them than I am!"

One dilemma is the ability of family members to feel an autonomous sense of accomplishment: It's hard to find your place in the sun, when you're in the shade of the family tree! Some family businesses solve this dilemma by giving each family member a different realm of responsibility. For example, David Chatham of Atlanta's Chatham Homes explains, "We've been able to distinguish ourselves in our fields without stepping on each other's toes, without being in the shadow of someone." In their case, the Chathams have one family member in a family owned bank, another heading up a landscape division, while others work in construction, interior design, etc.

Why So Complex?

Family businesses can be compared to a three-ring circus; each ring has its own activities, stars and equipment. In this case, the three systems include the family, the business and the individuals,

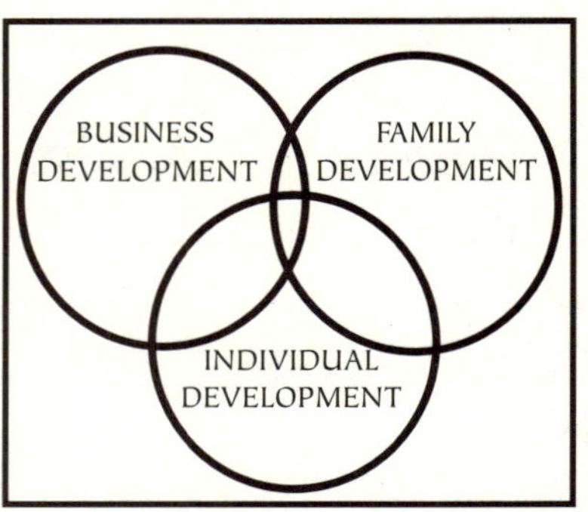

80

each with its own needs, goals and developmental stages. When all three systems are synchronized, conflict is at a minimum. However, it is rare that these systems are synchronized. Thus, the conflicting stages or needs become the challenges which family businesses and their advisors must resolve in order to maintain healthy businesses and families. Let's look at an example: The Smiths own a plumbing supply house. When they were first married, Mr. Smith was a plumber working for someone else. When he started his own business, Mrs. Smith helped by doing the books and answering the telephone. When their son was born, Mrs. Smith stayed home and Mr. Smith, who had another plumber and an apprentice working for him, hired an office manager. In the next five years, Mr. Smith added a plumbing supply division and the couple had another child. The business grew and Mrs. Smith occasionally helped out by pinch-hitting in the office or assisting with inventory. By the time the children were seven or eight years old,

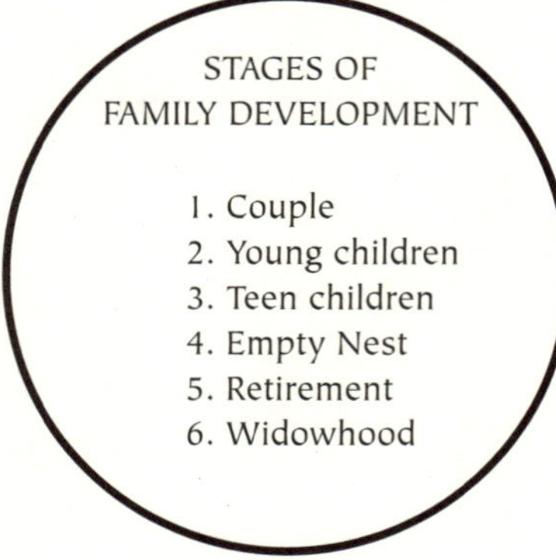

they would regularly come to the store and "help." During summer vacations, as the children grew older, their son would help the plumbers and their daughter helped at the supply counter, filling orders.

The son knew he wanted to follow in his father's footsteps, so he learned the plumbing trade by joining his father after high school. The daughter had little interest in the business and went on to college, helping out at the business to make extra money. When the children left home, Mrs. Smith began wondering what she could do next — and looked to the business for activity.

STAGES OF
ADULT INDIVIDUAL
DEVELOPMENT

Early adult transition (17-22)
Entering adult world (22-28)
Age 30 transition (28-33)
Settling down (33-40)
Mid-life transition (40-45)
Begin mid-adulthood (45-50)
Age 50 transition (50-55)
End mid-adulthood (55-60)
Late adult transition (60-65)
Late adulthood (65-80)

At this point, we can look at the family circle and see the "Empty Nest" stage: Mother, at forty-four, is in the mid-life transition (individual life stage), having completed her full-time job as mother, and is feeling a void. She looks to the business to fill this void, where there is presently no clear role for her.

Son, at twenty-three, wants to do things his own way, establishing himself as an autonomous adult. He is at the "Entering Adult World" stage of life. He seeks Dad's acceptance and more power to run the business, yet his competence to do so is in question.

Dad, at forty-eight, is entering "Middle Adulthood:" he doesn't quite trust his son's judgment yet, and thus is afraid to leave his "baby" (the business) in his son's hands. Like many entrepreneurs, Mr. Smith has a tremendous need to control his business and finds it difficult to trust others with it. He works long hours and rarely takes vacations.

The business's stage is moving towards "Delegation" from "Central Control": that is, the business is too big to be controlled solely at the top, requiring delegation, while controls must be established in order to allow the delegation to be handled responsibly and to allow for the comfort of the entrepreneur. As noted previously, entrepreneurs are not always good at letting go or at establishing systems.

Thus there are several points of conflict between the individual, family and business stages that create the conflicts experienced by Mr. Smith:

- The business needs systems and controls at its stage of development and none of the family (or employees) appears to be prepared to establish them.

- Father needs to delegate more but finds it difficult to do so since he lacks confidence in his son.

- The business requires outside assistance in order to move from this stage of development.

STAGES OF
BUSINESS DEVELOPMENT

Creativity — Leadership
Direction — Autonomy
Delegation — Control
Coordination — Red Tape
Collaboration — Regeneration

- The son feels stymied in his development by his father's retention of control and lack of confidence and is quite frustrated.

- He and Father bicker frequently, and Father feels his son is disrespectful and unappreciative (inter-generational and role conflict).

- Mother's development and the business's development are not in sync either. The business doesn't need an extra clerical person and Mother's skills are not appropriate elsewhere in the business. Here, Mr. Smith feels pulled: he puts Mrs. Smith on the payroll, but knows he's doing that as a husband, not as a good manager. This creates morale problems in the office which must be addressed.

The Smiths help us to understand how families in business together must keep their personal, family and business agendas clear and separate. When family business owners feel that the business must address all the family needs and the family must address all the business needs, none of the systems is very successful.

Guidelines for Staying Healthy in the Family Business

The following principles can assist family business leaders to create well-being in all three systems. These guidelines fall into four categories: integrity, clarity, respect and understanding.

- Integrity

The healthiest family businesses have a set of values by which they operate their lives and businesses. They steadfastly maintain these values. The company's reputation (and often its success) is based upon the quality that is anchored in these values.

The members of the family also demonstrate integrity in their clear sense of identity as part of and apart from the business. They are proud of their affiliation with the family and the business, and they have other interests as well. The integrity or wholeness of the individual is essential to the health of all three systems.

❧ Clarity

Integrity is facilitated by clarity of roles, rules and boundaries. Clarity of roles refers to the importance of clear expectations (often via written job descriptions) for the roles to be performed by each family employee.

Related to roles are interpersonal boundaries. It is important that each family member has a strong sense of his/her own identity, role at work and role at home and that all of these roles are clearly defined and respected by each other. "Clear Boundaries" also refers to the lines that are drawn between home and office: family issues should be discussed at home, business issues at work.

Finally, leaders of the healthy family business establish clear rules for how business is conducted, how family members can join the business, etc. These rules help create an atmosphere of trust, equity and professionalism.

❧ Respect

Involvement in the family business must be based upon mutual respect, not just kinship. When a family member enters the business without that respect, it is a set-up for conflict, lowered morale and self-esteem. For this reason, we advise that relatives who join the business bring their own portfolio of talents that are needed by this business. Children should work elsewhere before earning full-time employment in the family firm. This generally increases their respect for the parents' way of doing business as well as making the child more valuable to the business.

One manifestation of respect is shared power. The strongest family businesses have leaders who are able to share power because of the trust and respect they hold for others in the firm. (Note: "Shared" does not mean "equal.")

In addition, respect is demonstrated for each relative's autonomy, privacy and individuality.

Finally, families who respect themselves and the business recognize that they must carefully maintain the "three-cycle engine" of family, business and individual. They spend time asking questions such as "how are we doing as a team?" "Are we achieving our individual, family and business goals?" They spend time learning and growing together as well as utilizing other organizational development strategies to maintain the well-being of this complex system. In other words, they continually show respect for the complexity of the overlapping systems.

❧ Understanding

The final guideline to healthy family life in business is to work at mutual understanding. This understanding is based on genuine concern and love for one another as well as the aforementioned respect.

The skills or talents required in order to understand are listening and patience. If family members carefully listen to one another with the goal of understanding (rather than judging), misunderstanding and destructive conflict are minimized. Thorough, consistent, open, multidirectional communication is an essential key to success in any business — and particularly in the family business.

One aspect of the family business that is often overlooked is that segment of the family that is not active in or employed by the business. It is very important that they, too, understand what is happening in the family firm so that they can be supportive of those efforts and to prevent them from feeling like outsiders at family gatherings.

86

The Crisis of Families Who Work Together

Working with one's relatives can be filled with crises: crises within the family, in the business and/or in the personal lives of individuals. The Chinese have a wonderful way of looking at "crisis": their symbol for this concept includes one character signifying "danger," another signifying "opportunity." The challenges or dangers of working with one's family are great, as are the opportunities and payoffs. With careful attention to all three systems and reverence for the delicate balance one must maintain, families can work miracles together.

Chinese symbol for "crisis."

THE FAMILY BUSINESS QUIZ

Answer the following questions (true or false) regarding your own family's firm (or one for whom you work) or your own family system. Discuss your responses with others in the family and determine together the areas needing attention.

INTEGRITY

1. Our family values are clearly articulated and are observable in our decisions, policies and day-to-day interactions.

 * Bonus Point: We have a written family charter or statement of philosophy.

2. Most members of the family team have a clear, comfortable sense of their individual identities, beliefs and interests.

CLARITY

3. Family members clearly understand what their roles are at work and at home and keep these separate.

4. There are accurate written job descriptions for each position in the company (for all family employees as well).

RESPECT

5. There are clear guidelines for how members of the family may join the business.

6. Authority and responsibility are delegated throughout the organization.

7. Key issues are discussed with other family employees before decisions are made.

8. We are "self-conscious" about our operations, i.e., we discuss how we are accomplishing our tasks and goals and meeting the needs of individuals and the business.

UNDERSTANDING

9. We spend more time trying to understand each others' perspectives than arguing for our own.

10. We regularly include family members who are not active in the business in discussions of company status.

87

20

Geometry of Family Business

We often use shapes to help explain the phenomenons we observe in family businesses. This chapter uses circles, squares, triangles and octagons to describe the dynamics (or perils and pleasures) of family business. You'll find here a series of guidelines to foster harmony and prosperity in the family business.

Challenges of Working in Family Businesses

Family businesses are tricky! Although there are estimates that they make up to 80-90% of all businesses in the United States and more than 60% of the GDP, it is very difficult to sustain family businesses over the generations. Although statistics are not well kept, it is estimated that only 39% reach the second generation and l5% make it to the third generation. Why is this?

Participants in my workshops and retreats share the dilemmas they face working and living with family businesses:

⚘ Separating work from personal issues.

I frequently hear problems like, "When my father criticizes my work at the office, it's hard for me to tell whether he's 'fathering me' or giving me real, objective supervision. So, I overreact, taking offense at his intruding our personal lives in the workplace."

⚘ Difficulty establishing a more formalized structure.

Many family business members have told me, "We're all used to pitching in and doing whatever it takes to build the business. No one has a formal job description. When we try to institute clear roles, responsibilities, accountabilities and lines of authority, many of the family members object, feeling it's too bureaucratic and arti-ficial. Yet confusion often arises over who is going to do what and things fall between the cracks. Non-family employees are some-times unclear about what they should or shouldn't do and are afraid of stepping on someone's toes. Sometimes we don't know who's in charge of what, who can make what decisions. Process improvement can be very difficult in this type of informal organiza-tion.

❧ Conflict.

Family members often find it difficult to negotiate differences in a constructive manner. Excessive sensitivity (or insensitivity) on a personal basis can lead to aggressive and passive-aggressive behavior. Unresolved personal conflicts get played out in the work-place, causing discomfort for family and non-family alike.

❧ Communicating with family members who are not in the business.

"They just don't understand," complains one brother-in-law, "how hard we work and what it takes to build the business. They want cash now and don't care if it means we can't build the capac-ity of the business for the future." Yet it takes a lot of time and energy to enlighten family members who are not in the business about the challenges, opportunities and needs of the business, so that they will be more supportive.

❧ Cannot leave work problems at work.

In a non-family business it is sometimes difficult to switch gears when you go home, to talk about other things. Going home with a co-worker who also happens to be your spouse makes it even more difficult to leave the problems outside the bedroom door. Family members not active in the business often complain that they feel left out of these conversations and that "No one ever talks about anything except the business!"

- Juggling family and business needs.

Although not unique to family businesses, many family business owners observe that the immense needs of a young, growing business often occur at the same time as those of young children. Young business owners often complain that "There is no one else to blame — no "boss" or "nameless corporate devil." I have to take the responsibility of saying to the kids that I can't be at their game because of I have to take care of our business."

- Differences in perspectives between generations

The generation gap rears its ugly head in many ways in the family business. As we get older we often get conservative, just when the younger generation wants to get their hands on the reigns to try something new. In many situations, the older generation sacrificed a lot for the business, including time with the children. The younger generation typically wants more "balance" in life and as such seems ungrateful or not willing to make the commitment that the business needs. "They don't have the same work ethic as we had," worry older family members, "and that concerns us about the viability of the business."

Advantages of Family Business

So why do people invite family members to join them in business and/or decide to make the plunge and come into the family business? There are still many advantages:

- The opportunity to spend time with family members and to share a common interest.

With families becoming so dispersed in this day and age, having the business in common helps us to stay connected. We can also have a shared experience: both shared struggles and success. Opportunity to learn from each other is also a motivator for becoming involved in family businesses. It can be like the old-fashioned "apprenticeship" with those people whom we respect.

❧ Flexibility in one's own business.

Typically family businesses provide more flexibility, because the business is a means of financial support and constructive occupation. So other personal needs (time off for kids, education or other needs) are easier to accommodate. Further, kids get to learn more aspects of a business than if they joined a large, non-family corporation where they may be slotted into a more specialized role.

❧ Chance to perpetuate the business.

A major goal for many entrepreneurs is to find a way to continue the business beyond their active working life. Family members in the business give some assurance that the emotional commitment will be there to maintain their legacy. In fact, more and more we are finding that the younger generation feels a sense of loyalty and pride in the family business and so seeks the opportunity to help perpetuate it.

❧ Working with people you trust and having "backup" you can count on.

Family members are often invested in the long-term success of the business, so they watch the shop more closely than someone who is not related. That is the motivation for many business owners to make their entrepreneurial ventures family businesses.

Solving/Avoiding These Problems: Complex Systems

Here are some geometric guidelines for healthy family businesses:

❧ Keep your circles separate.

  ❧ In studying family businesses, we often represent the family by one circle and the business by another: each is a unique system, with different rules, roles and expectations. When the systems overlap each other, the result is often confusion and conflict...

    ❧ Give family members a chance in the family business if they have the ability or potential to contribute to the business.

OVERLAPPING SYSTEMS

FAMILY SYSTEM

1. Emotion-focused.
2. Inward-oriented.
3. Minimizes change.
4. Unconditional acceptance.

Tasks:
Nurture
Develop self-esteem
Grow Adults

BUSINESS SYSTEM

1. Rational-focused.
2. Outward-oriented.
3. Requires change.
4. Conditional acceptance.

Tasks:
Generate profits
Develop skills

92

❧ Spend time with family members, nurturing those relationships outside of the business.

❧ Establish a written policy about family employment so that everyone understands the terms of entering, staying and leaving the business.

❧ Have annual family retreats so that family members not working in the business have a common picture of the issues and benefits of this important family entity.

❧ Keep your squares permeable, but not with gaping holes.

❧ Permeability of interpersonal boundaries allows us to take in the perspectives, reactions and needs of others. If our boundaries are too permeable, we lose our own integrity and sense of self.

❧ Listen openly to the ideas and feedback of others, and recognize that they are sharing their own perspectives.

❧ Be assertive in checking out your understanding of another person's perspective, to assure you have an accurate picture. (Don't assume.)

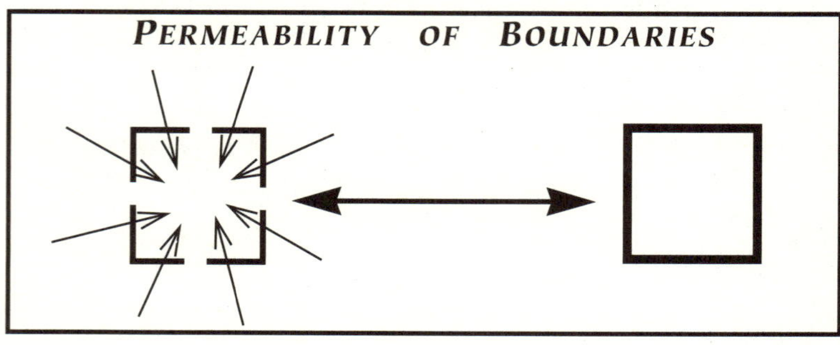

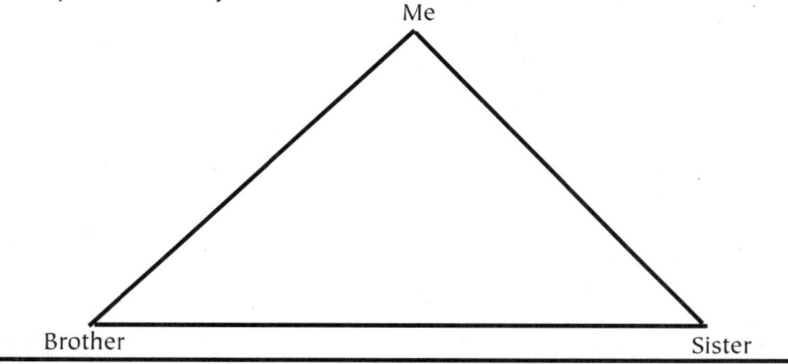

FAMILY TRIANGLES

Communication should happen directly between individuals, not through others. For example, when I am asked by Sister to "tell our brother off," she is asking me to get in the middle of a triangle. If I get angry at Brother for her, and "tell him off," I am creating a triangle and keeping them from solving their problems directly.

- ❧ Stay out of triangles.

  - ❧ Communication triangles occur when two parties are in conflict and a third gets in the middle to try to solve the problem, rather than encouraging the two involved to fix it themselves.

    - ❧ Listen with empathy when someone ventilates about a problem with a third party, but don't jump in the middle.

    - ❧ Be a coach: help the person who is coming to you to give constructive feedback to the third party.

    - ❧ Remember that the person in the middle often "gets shot" by both sides and just perpetuates the dysfunction of the relationship.

- ❧ Octagon.

  - ❧ There are many sides to every story.

  - ❧ *Seek to understand, not to judge.*

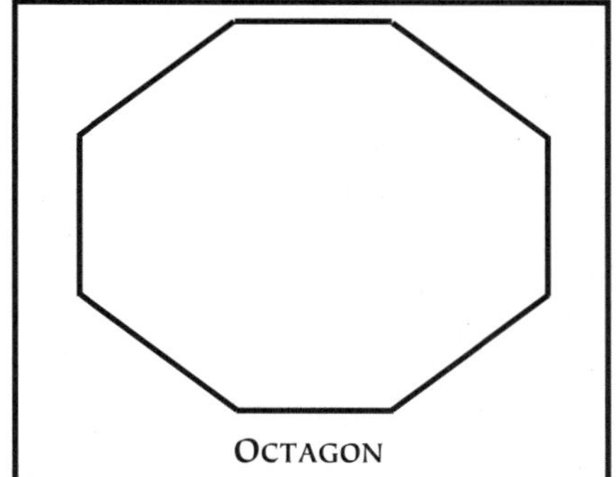

21

THE LION KING:
THE CHALLENGE OF FAMILY BUSINESS SUCCESSION

In 1994 a wonderful movie was released about family succession issues, entitled The Lion King. *Now, you may not have realized that it offered a close parallel to the human family business world, but I noticed it immediately! In fact, it was one of the few children's movies I voluntarily attended more than once with my daughter! We drew some important lessons on family businesses from this film.*

"A king's time as a ruler rises and sets like the sun," the father teaches his son (and successor). "Remember who you are."

These words seem like sound advice from a father to a son or, as in this case, from a lion to his cub. Yet *The Lion King* is truly a story out of the pages of a family business succession story, reflecting the many challenges of choosing a successor, jealousy of the uncle who wasn't anointed as the leader, death and loss, the journey of separation and individuation of the younger generation and the rightful passage to become the leader when "It is time." Even the musical theme, appropriately enough, was called *The Circle of Life.*

For those of you who haven't been drawn to the theater by one of your "successors," this Disney movie begins with the birth of Simba to Mufasa, the King of Pride Rock. Simba is proudly presented to the kingdom as the successor to the throne. His uncle "Scar" does not share the kingdom's joy, as this infant "hairball" is the barrier to Scar's ascension to the throne. Scar plots with the enemy hyenas to overthrow the crown and take it for himself.

So as not to destroy the movie for those who have not yet seen it, I will not describe more of the plot, but let me share the challenges and comments which struck me as parallel to the human story: all members of family businesses could learn some lessons from this animal kingdom.

"Shallow End of the Gene Pool"

The king's younger brother covets his brother's position and describes himself as the one with the brains, while Mufasa, the Lion King, got the brawn: "When it comes to brute strength, I was in the shallow end of the gene pool." Scar points to the persistence of primogeniture, i.e. that the oldest male gets everything, whether or not he's the best choice for the job. Family businesses can learn from Scar and move past this ancient English tradition, by developing a clear picture of the leadership needs of the business and the family and select the best candidate, whatever their gender or birth order.

"I Just Can't Wait to Be King"

The song, sung, of course, by Simba the successor, points to the sense of immortality and risk-taking of the next generation. After being rescued from near death by his father, Simba walks downcast behind the king, putting his small paws in the large tracks of his father's footprints. He gains some humility in the process...and looks for assurance from dad that he will always be there for him. Dad shares some of his philosophy with Simba, which had been passed down from his own father: "Son, I may not always be here for you but if you look in the sky, at those sparkling lights, you will see me. My father said that when kings die, they pass on and become the stars in the sky." Mufasa illustrates the importance of tradition, shared beliefs and legacy, which we have

95

found characterizes the families who stay positively connected and continue to work productively together in a family business.

"Hakuna Matata"

Adolescents go through a difficult time of wanting to be grown up and yet fearing the responsibility of adulthood. When adulthood is prematurely thrust upon Simba, he runs. Despondent, he gives up and is adopted by a new "peer group" who teaches him a new philosophy: "Hakuna Matata," meaning "No worries." He later described this period of time as giving him the opportunity to become his own person...not just a reflection of his dad, and maybe not the failure his uncle described. When his crisis peaked, he roared at his late father, "You said you'd always be there for me, but you're not!," completing the mourning and adolescent separation he needed to grow up.

When human beings are thrust into the family business before establishing their own identity and sense of competence elsewhere, they often have several problems. First, they may find it difficult to gain a sense of their own worth and/or appreciation for what they have to offer as competent professionals. Secondly, when mom or dad plays the role of "boss," the child may react to this as parenting rather than appropriate managerial guidance. Time away sometimes yields perspective on the range of behaviors one finds in non-family businesses and can foster an appreciation of one's parents' capabilities.

Rafiki, the Family Business Consultant

Feeling like a failure, certainly not the lion his father was, Simba is reluctant to live up to the challenge of succession. Rafiki, the baboon who has been his father's trusted advisor, finds Simba and takes him on an uncomfortable journey to discover himself. With Rafiki's help, Simba hears his father's admonition that "You are more than you have become....remember who you are." As he gathers the strength to return to his kingdom, he says to Rafiki, "It looks like the winds are changing." Rafiki replies, "Ah, change is good" (sounding like most family business consultants). To which Simba responds, "Yeah, but it's hard."

The roadblocks to success in family businesses are often of a personal and developmental nature. Family business consultants are often called upon to assist in providing coaching, facilitating growth and exploring new paths "through the jungle" of family conflict.

97

Zazu Observes Different Management Styles

The faithful non-family employee, the bird Zazu, comments on the fact that the incumbents of the throne during his tenure have had differing management styles. Zazu was an outsider — not a member of the family — who had some clarity about the situation, but who wasn't taken very seriously by the royal family. Was he articulate? Did he take a strong position or action? Or were his views truly considered by the family? Often managers in family businesses who do not share the owners' last name feel disenfranchised. Listening well to key employees and assuring their sense of security can be critical to the long-term health of a family business.

Leadership and Vision

"We're talking kings and succession," speaks Scar at one point to a groups of hyenas. He shares his vision for the kingdom, should he become king. "Stick with me and you'll never go hungry." And he gives a compelling case for each individual's role in achieving that vision (i.e., killing the current king). He also shares a guiding principle ("Be prepared"). His intentions may be destructive, but he knows how to be a successful leader: state a clear vision, enroll individuals in that vision, show their role in accomplishing it and give them principles to follow in the process. However, his lack of integrity, as well as his failure to fulfill his part of the deal, eventually catch up with him and destroy the commitment of his followers.

It Is Time: Celebration of Renewal

The journey to succession doesn't always follow the timetable that either generation expects...typically, it is not as fast as the younger generation hopes or as smooth as the older might like. Sometimes, it requires an interim manager while the younger generation matures. When the time comes, as it did in this movie, it is cause for a celebration of the renewal which the transition represents. Rafiki presides at the ceremony and is even there to present the next generation to the community. The theme *The Circle of Life* plays at the end to emphasize this renewal. The continuity of the successor, as well as the wisdom that is passed down, assures the immortality of the parent.

Rituals are important and often neglected in our fast-paced, task-oriented world. Yet rituals, such as the passing of a gavel, help to mark a transition and assist participants to make the psychological adjustments which accompany a change in leadership and power.

Some may say that the lessons from "Lion King" represent pretty conventional wisdom about family business. I say the movie offers reflective audiences who live and work in family businesses the opportunity to consider their own transition processes and can provide a family with a wonderful conversation starter![1]

---

1. Thanks to my daughter, Baleigh Dashew Isaacs, for her assistance on this chapter. Another version of this piece was published in *Family Business* magazine.

22

CONTINUITY AND SUCCESSION:
FAMILY BUSINESS AND THE NEXT GENERATION

Determining how the family business will continue beyond the current generation is one of the major turning points for family businesses. The "older" generation often has trouble trusting the "younger" generation with the care and feeding of the "baby" called the "business." The younger generation struggles with the question of whether there is an appropriate role in the family business and whether they want to take one. This chapter describes the viewpoints of a number of these younger folks.

As family business consultants, we often hear about the frustrations of the younger generation: they feel that the "older generation" does not understand their dilemmas nor the need for new ideas, new ways of doing business, etc. The anthropologist Margaret Mead understood this dilemma and her perspective is as relevant to family businesses as it is to aboriginal families. She described the importance of a dialogue among three generations: the oldest generation to describe how things used to be (heritage); the middle generation to describe how things are (current realities); and the younger generation to describe how things can be (future vision).

In a recent meeting with a number of young people in successor generations, we heard of their struggles, achievements and principles for success. The following are some observations and stories for that discussion.

One interesting observation was that the women in family businesses, by and large, had worked outside the family business for some time before coming in, as opposed to the men who went directly into the business.

One woman was in the hotel business. Her father didn't believe girls should be in the business as professionals, but should be groomed as wives. She went to finishing school and while there secretly enrolled in a university program to learn about finance. She returned to her hometown and went to work for a competing hotel chain. Her father asked why she didn't come to work for them and she explained her understanding of his expectations. His distaste for a family member working for a competitor and his daughter's training (which was valuable to the family business) was enough to make him rethink his beliefs about women in the family business. The young woman came to have a key role in financial management and later in general management of the hotel holdings.

Another young woman never thought about working in the family clothing manufacturing business as a viable option. Her brothers were encouraged to join and to take a leadership role in the business. She went to work in sales and marketing in a different industry. Eventually her family realized the talents she had and encouraged her to put them to work for the family. As she worked in the family business, succession plans were made. Her eldest brother was designated as the person to take the lead. However, her brothers saw that she had the combination of people skills and business knowledge which neither of them possessed and they have now encouraged her to take the lead.

A third young woman thought the family candy business was too small and was not of interest to her. She went to law school and worked in environmental advocacy roles. However, the pull of her grandfather and his legacy was strong. She joined the family business to stay connected with the family. Although she doesn't have a role that formally capitalizes on her legal training, the training has served her in two ways: first, her professional credentials once again impressed the family and made them take a second look at "the little girl" as a potential contributor to the business. Second, the family draws upon her legal expertise when licensing or other matters require legal advice. Although she doesn't practice law on behalf of the family business, she advises them on strategy and helps select appropriate counsel.

The family business successors described their challenges in the following ways:

* Maintaining our own identity while working in the family business.

* Making our own mark on the business: a unique contribution which continues the success of the business.

* Feeling OK about making mistakes (and not feeling like you have to be perfect, because the family is looking over your shoulder).

* Addressing the differing agendas of siblings regarding management of the family assets (e.g., keep the business vs. sell).

* Mediating the differing philosophies of three generations, particularly regarding how much risk to take.

* Feeling the pressure of keeping the business alive for another generation when the failure rate is so high for third generation businesses.

* Gaining credibility with employees, suppliers and customers as a viable business person, and not just "the boss' kid" or "a girl".

* Balancing what worked in the past (and sometimes what made the company unique) with new ideas, perspectives and ventures.

❧ Finding a way to keep the family connected when "grandma" (the "chief emotional officer") can no longer play that role and the family is growing and spreading out.

When asked about some of the strategies which they have found help to keep the family business strong and harmonious, the young people shared the following observations:

❧ A strong commitment to maintain and grow the family business, to be the best.

❧ The preservation of stability and tradition.

❧ Desire to stay connected to the family and maintain a "sense of family."

❧ Balance between new ideas and respect for the lessons of the past.

❧ Flexibility and the willingness to compromise.

❧ Business knowledge and the knowledge of this business.

❧ Having a vision of what the business can be.

I was impressed with the wisdom of this group of young people: they recognized the importance of the past and the present while they also sought new solutions which would bring the business successfully into another generation. This is certainly good news for family business!

103

23

FINDING THE WORK OF YOUR LIFE: AND WHAT IF IT ISN'T IN THE FAMILY BUSINESS?

I find that people of all ages struggle with the existential issues of their purpose in life and their ideal occupation. This is often more difficult in family businesses as young people must also decide whether or not to be in the family business and how this will effect the rest of the family. The following chapter addresses this issue and offers suggestions for those in the struggle as well as those around them.

It is Thanksgiving and I am sitting with the family in Tucson. My niece, Sarah, is discussing the preparations of her boat for her sail to the South Pacific. Her sister, Elyse, is working with her dad (my brother) on the latest version of their cruising book (of which she is in charge of production and distribution).[1] Grandfather, Father and Mother are assisting Sarah with ideas as she prepares to go to sea. Both daughters are following in the family path of sailing and/or writing.

On the other coast, my niece and nephew are discussing via telephone their consulting and clinical practice with me, asking for my advice and counsel in fields related to my work. They, too, follow family careers in medicine, counseling and consulting.

---

1. The same niece, Elyse Dashew, is currently in charge of the production and publication of *The Best of the Human Side.*

How nice it is to see kids grow and develop and to be able to help them because of their shared interests in the work of their lives. But how do you know if the family business is the Work of Your Life? How do you help children find their passion?

Finding One's Self, One's Purpose

People from all cultures typically begin struggling with their identity and purpose at puberty. The adolescent stage of separation and individuation is sometimes more difficult to complete in the family business environment. A teenager's job is to find his or her "identity" as an individual, separate from that of the parents. In families where the business and the family are merged and both feel ever-present to the teen, it is more difficult to step aside and look at one's own interests. Kids can feel that following the family footsteps is the only acceptable way. Some do that and are happy. Others do so and never "actualize themselves." Still others (often the youngest members of the family) leave home, thinking that distance is the only way to find themselves. Others rebel and go in a direction that is nothing like that of the family.

When teens have the space and time to explore multiple paths or identities, they most often settle into one that is congruent with the values of the family. The key is having the space, time and support to do the exploration.

Several Native American tribes have a tradition of the "Vision Quest." As members of the younger generation face adulthood, they are sent off to travel on their own and gain insight (or a "vision") about their individual purpose in life. Once they successfully complete the quest, they are welcomed back as adult members of the tribe.

In the Bedouin Tuareg Tribe in West Africa, the father gives a cross to his son to help him find his path. Similar to the Native Americans, the son is sent into bush at puberty for one month to find himself. Father says to Son: "Life is short. I don't know what path you will take, North, South, East or West, but I wish you a good life and good fortune."

The result of the adolescent passage into adulthood is, ideally, an understanding of one's purpose in life. One way of crystallizing this purpose is to create a "mission statement" for one's self. With this sense of purpose or mission in mind, it is easier to determine what occupation would help us to achieve our mission in life.

During the next stage of growth, one must have a sense of accomplishment (industriousness) to feel good about oneself. The sense of purpose becomes the course we take, and our ability to make progress on that path gives us that sense of accomplishment.

Thus, in order to foster strong self-esteem, it is important to find work that is meaningful, makes a contribution, and/or is productive. The ideal is to explore different types of work that also add value to the organization.

The Happiest People Are Those Who Know What They Love to Do and Do It

Years ago, I met a young man who was in dental school and was having serious heart problems at his young age. His family wanted him to be a dentist and have a secure financial future. They sacrificed to make his education possible, and he felt obliged to carry out his family's wishes. On the side, he began an antique and auction business and loved it. Finally, he decided that his passion was the antique business and quit dental school. When he next went for check up and treatment, they found no signs of his well-documented heart problems. They tested and retested him and, to their amazement, found nothing. I believe, as did he, that his heart problems were a result of trying to be someone else or follow a path that wasn't his own.

The happiest people are those who know what they love to do and do it. Many people contend (in books such as *Do What You Love and The Money Will Follow*[1]) that financial success is also tied to finding your passion or purpose and working at it.

1. Sinetar, Marsha. *Do What You Love and the Money Will Follow: Discovering Your Right Livelihood.* Dell Books. 1990.

Parents in family businesses often tell me that they have told their kids to do what they want and not to feel obligated to join the family business. This is particularly true of those parents who felt compelled to join the family business themselves and had "golden handcuffs" that kept them there despite their lack of passion.

Yet some young people struggle to determine what they want to do and look at the family business as a safe and available option. Others, sensing their parents' lack of direction, feel their confusion and anxiety and find it more difficult to leave and develop their own direction. Thus, it is important that all members of the family be clear about their own purpose and share that with the younger generation.

In the healthiest family businesses, there is an evolution or development which occurs within individual members, in the family as a whole and in the business: what I refer to as co-evolution of the three components of the family business. However, we often find that the evolution of the business occurs at the expense of the individuals and/or the family. At times, the family evolves at the expense of the business or individuals. Paying attention to the growth of each component is essential to the health of the entire system.

Help for People Trying to Decide What to Do When They "Grow Up"

Many families struggle with how to help a member of the family determine his purpose or passion (or even how to help ourselves!).

Although developmentally this is an adolescent issue, sometimes we find adults of all ages who have not addressed this challenge until much later in life. Here are some suggestions:

❋ First, be sure that you are clear about your own purpose and are communicating that (through words and deeds) to those around you.

❦ Second, encourage your family members to create his own statement of purpose, such as a mission statement. One helpful way to begin organizing thoughts about one's purpose is to think about death. For what would you want to be remembered after you have died? If you have lived a very fulfilling life, what would you have done and how would you have impacted people around you? Provide access to relationships (e.g., opportunity to talk about options as a coach, rather than as an advocate for a position) through which to explore direction and opportunities.

❦ Make sure that a clear message is projected that you and the business will be fine no matter what the young person does.

❦ Help him look at his interests by thinking about his behavior: What excites him? What does he do with any free time? What draws his attention? What does he deem important or value in life? What does he read or watch on television?

❦ Help him identify his capabilities in terms of specific skills and knowledge (not in terms of jobs or occupations, but in terms of specific activities — e.g., writing, collecting information, taking photos, organizing activities, taking apart and putting together radios, teaching, coaching, meeting people easily, working with numbers, manual dexterity, etc.).

❦ Then he should look at preferences such as how much stimulation from other people he needs in his work, as opposed to working by himself. What kind of information does he naturally notice — details, or the big picture? What factors are most important in coming to decisions — personally held values and harmony or logic and precedent? Finally, how does he prefer to live his life — in a structured and organized manner or more spontaneously? All of these factors help to determine what kinds of jobs or careers will give the individual satisfaction.

❦ You might even share your assumptions about his interests: what you have observed in their behavior.

❧ Books such as *What Color is Your Parachute*[1] help to cluster interests, abilities, work environment and lifestyle preferences to identify possible occupations and careers.

❧ If possible, offer access to career counselors who can provide a battery of tests to explore career directions in more depth.

❧ Give them time to explore themselves and learn what matters to them, without the heavy influence of family members.

109

And what if they decide not to work in the family business?

If their explorations take them elsewhere and not toward work in the family business...how do you handle it? Celebrate with them that they have found their joy...maybe even their dream. Realize that our children cannot make our dreams come true; only we can.

AN EXERCISE TO HELP YOU CREATE YOUR OWN MISSION STATEMENT

Imagine your own funeral three years from now and imagine that between now and then you have lived the most fulfilling life you can imagine (no need to know specifics). Now imagine four people that you know participating in your eulogy: one from your family, one from your friends, one from your work life, and one from your community. Imagine them talking about how your life (in the last three years) influenced theirs in meaningful ways. As you imagine their statements jot down the words they use to describe you and how you effected them. Sit with these descriptions until you distill a single-sentence life's purpose statement that would create the effects on others that your four people described.[2]

1.Bolles, Richard Nelson. *What Color Is Your Parachute: A Practical Manual for Job Hunters and Career Changers.* Ten Speed Press. 1995.
2. Submitted by Joe Paul as adapted from Covey Materials.

24

JOINING THE FAMILY BUSINESS

Another common issue for families in business is how to assure fairness of employment to the members of the family and appropriate employees working in the business. This chapter describes a set of criteria which families should consider in developing policies on family employment.

The Challenge

"Dad always wanted me to join the business and spoke as if there were no other choices for me," said one young man "I sometimes wonder if this is the best thing for me....but I've been here since high school and I don't know if I could get hired anywhere else."

A young woman in her thirties described a different set of circumstances. "My grandfather founded our business and never considered the possibilities that his "girls" would join the business. But when my father and uncles began looking at our generation of 6-8 kids who could be employed by the business, they decided we should all have the chance. I wasn't at all interested in joining the business. However, after I finished graduate school, it seemed almost disloyal not to use my skills within the family. Now I feel like I got the job because of my ability, not just my family ties."

"Well, I'm really frustrated!" chimed in a third discussant. "I worked my way up to a management position in our business after six years here. Now, they've brought in my cousin who has no experience and he's getting the same salary I'm getting. They said they feel that all of us in the family should earn the same amount. But he's not contributing his share to the bottom line!"

The above group of young business people joined their families' businesses over the past several years. Discussing problems, they have encountered as son, daughter, spouse or nephew of the founder or current company leader helps them to reflect on how the decision was made for them to join the family business.

Strategies for Successful Resolution

All of these family employees are learning to cope with the dilemmas that arise when family members join a business. The overlapping roles, expectations and values of each system (family and business) often create conflicts for family members who try to take care of their business and family responsibilities simultaneously. The most constructive route to balancing these responsibilities, opportunities and needs is to develop clear and separate statements of mission for the family and the business. The business may be an asset that furthers the mission of the family, rather than a source of conflict and unhappiness in both realms.

A second strategy that helps to maintain harmony in the family and success in the business is the development of a set of guidelines for entry into the family business. In essence, these guidelines can provide structure and objectivity to decisions which can be emotionally-laden and full of uncomfortable ramifications such as those discussed in the first paragraphs. The rules for entry can be a concrete manifestation of complementary family and business mission statements.

Developing Guidelines for Entry

There do not appear to be any "golden rules" of entry into family businesses. In canvassing many professional family business advisors and reviewing the family business literature, the prevalent rule is to have a clear policy of family employment and to be relatively consistent (no pun intended) in the use of these guidelines. The nature of the guidelines depends in part on the nature of the family and business, as well as their missions, size, industry and resources available.

There does seem to be some consistency in what areas to include in the guidelines:

Who Is Eligible to Join the Business?

Some family businesses limit employment to non-family members, believing that this strategy eliminates most conflicts while maintaining ownership of the business as an asset to benefit family members. Other choices include whether to offer employment to spouses, uncles-in-laws or cousins by marriage. If the criteria are clear and the other five areas below are defined specifically, possible problems with nepotism can be avoided. (Nepotism is defined as the advancement of a relative on the basis of family ties rather than merit.)

Most advisors feel that family members should not be hired solely because of their kinship. They must have the ability or potential to contribute to the business.

At What Point Are They Eligible to Join?

There is much conventional wisdom about the point at which family members can join the firm:

* Age.

Most sources support exposure of youngsters to the business through summer jobs in high school. Entry immediately after high school (or college) is discouraged by most people with experience in this field. Phil Sidwell[1], a 20-year veteran in family business consulting, believes that a 21-year-old generally does not have suf-

---

1. Private communication.

ficient maturity to handle the web of dilemmas often presented by the family dynamics and business stressors in a family-owned business. Some of Sidwell's criteria for maturity include: a strong sense of one's own identity and competency, willingness to learn, comfort with independence and interdependence and a fair amount of objectivity.

Some advisors suggest age limits by which time a family member must join the business, should they wish that opportunity. This policy encourages long term commitment, rather than providing a security blanket if all else fails.

❧ Experience.

Experience seems to be a more generally accepted criteria for family business entry than any specific educational base. Sybil Ferguson, the founder of The Diet Center, involved many family members in her business. Her 20/20 hind-sight included the value of working elsewhere prior to joining the family business. She suggested a minimum of two years of work outside the business. John Ward[1], John Davis[2] and David Bork[3], along with many other well-known family business experts, believe three to five years of experience on one's own is essential. Bork describes six dimensions of this experience:

❧ *Three to five years of employment in a job or jobs that have depended on competence, skill and sustained performance, rather than on family-based relationships.*

❧ *At least one of those jobs should have lasted two years or more and included promotion. (Two years in a job is ample opportunity to demonstrate competence and earn promotion.)*

---

1. Ward, John. *Keeping the Family Business Healthy.* San Francisco: Jossey-Bass. 1987.
2. Davis, John. *Family Business Review.* Volume 1, #4, p.421.
3. Bork, David. *Family Business, Risky Business.* New York: Amacom. 1986.

> *Experience in directing the activities of others.*

> *Recognition for demonstrated competence in the job.*

> *Evidence of ability and willingness to take initiative on the job.*

> *Evidence of having been a valued employee with legitimate contributions to make[1].*

114

The outside business experience benefits the individuals by developing their business competence and confidence and it benefits their family business through the enhanced contribution the new family employee can make. This contribution is enhanced if the business is larger (Sidwell[2] suggests a multiplier of five times the family business volume; Ward[3] suggests that it be of the size the family business hopes to attain) and the family employee can learn more sophisticated strategies to share with his family. In other words, "He can go to school at the other guy's expense."

> Education.

Education level depends upon the needs of the business. Although it seems that many experts recommend a college education, many others suggest that this may be a family value, rather than a business need. In any case, the criteria for entry into the business probably should relate to the needs of the business. If the business interest would be advanced by a well-trained professional (accountant, attorney, engineer), then this need may be reflected accordingly. On the other hand, an over-trained employee (family or otherwise) can create morale problems. Gratifying opportunities for an attorney in a two million dollar plumbing equipment company would be limited. Sidwell believes appropriate training or educational experience can be found in areas other than college: the military, technical training and/or structured professional training programs in other companies.

---

1. Bork, David. *ibid.*
2. Personal correspondence.
3. Ward, John. *ibid.*

With What Commitment?

Some family businesses have begun with Dad and/or Mom holding down a full-time job and growing the family business on a very part-time basis. The part-time employment may continue to address family needs (e.g., a parent who wants to be at home with children). At some point in the development of the business, professionalism and full-time commitment may be necessary to reach new levels of profitability and competitiveness. Once again, the size, values of the family and the marketplace are considerations in developing a policy.

One way of handling this issue is to develop a multiple-track family employment model. For instance, one track would allow youngsters or new in-laws to "sample" the family business to determine long-range career interests. This approach allows exposure to the potential rewards as well as challenges of joining the family business, prior to making a major commitment. Many families provide this opportunity through summer employment or part-time work during college. A second option would be a leadership track in which the family employee and the company have chosen each other with the ultimate goal of providing leadership to the family business (as CEO or other key roles). This track includes special criteria for membership (e.g., education requirements, apprenticeships, experience within and outside the business, etc.) and includes a clear plan of development and progression within the firm. Obviously the mutual commitment in this track is quite high.

A third track would be for the family employees who have skills that could be utilized by the firm and who would work in any case, but who may be neither interested in nor capable of leadership. An example of someone on this path is the son's wife who has worked outside of the business as a secretary. She would like to work in the family business to feel more connected to the family and involved in her husband's life. The company can use the clerical support as well as an employee who has high investment in the success of the company.

Other considerations for policy are whether family members who leave the business are eligible for rehire and under what conditions (e.g., leave for pregnancy or education vs. quitting over family conflict).

To Do What?

Most of the advisors in the family business arena (including family business owners) warn against creating unnecessary positions in order to employ a family member. This creates resentment among other employees and does little for the self-esteem of the incumbent. The conventional wisdom is to only offer a position that meets a clear need in the organization, for which the candidate is clearly qualified (after all, that makes good business sense!). The only partial exception to that rule is the apprenticeship of a successor who may move from position to position or project to project in order to learn many aspects of the business. Even in that case, the family employee's creditability and acceptance will be more readily developed if he or she is making an obvious contribution to the firm.

Finally, there are times when a position may be created for a family member who, for instance, has worked in a specialist role elsewhere and can advance the firm's capability by providing assistance in a new role. In this case the custom-made job clearly advances the interest of the business as well as the family member.

With What Assistance or Supervision?

Once family members are hired, who supervises them and what training opportunities are offered to them? More times than not, this is handled informally and thus less effectively than with a more structured, objective approach. A second strategy is to have the employee report to a non-family supervisor. This policy decreases the subjectivity of evaluations and feedback and the probability of over-emotionality.

Training for family members, particularly those aiming for leadership roles, is often more intense or extensive than for non-family employees. Once again, the consensus of opinion is suggestive of structure: look objectively at the intended role(s) of the family employee and design learning opportunities (education plus experience), that will optimally prepare him/her over a reasonable period of time. This approach typically includes increasing levels of responsibility and autonomy to allow the family employee to gain confidence and better judgment.

Finally, it is advised that whenever possible the family employee have a designated mentor or coach (outside of the immediate family) who can provide industry-specific guidance as well as candid feedback to the family employee. The mentor is particularly important for the family employee on the leadership track. In smaller family firms, the parent (or other family leader) is often mentor-by-default: unconsciously providing a role model and messages about how to conduct business.

At times, the model is neither ideal nor what the mentor-by-fault would choose to have the newcomer follow. Thus, the more deliberate the plan of development (including open discussion of the newcomer's perceptions) the greater the potential to learn constructive lessons.

Under What Condition of Employment?

One family-business owner described their policy: "We can hire family members, but immediate supervisors are authorized to fire them!" Family members often get "an extra chance" not afforded other employees. However, if this practice becomes pervasive, it gives destructive messages to everyone, such as "We really don't hold everyone accountable" or "Unless you're a family member, don't expect good treatment." Both messages undermine productivity, morale and stability of the work force.

On the other hand, children in family businesses often complain that they are expected to work harder, for less immediate compensation than all other employees. "My brother told me that I must always get to work at least fifteen minutes before all the other employees and stay at least fifteen minutes after the last one leaves!"

By and large, family business advisors suggest that a family member who does not maintain minimum standards of performance should not be kept on payroll. It is very hard to expect other employees to buy into tight budget constraints when they see family members wasting time and company resources. Similarly, most advisors suggest that companies pay market value for all jobs and compensate family members through dividends, bonuses, or other outside compensation.

Successful Strategies/Successful Businesses

The advice from management consultants and business schools up until 10-15 years ago was: "If you want a successful family business, bring in "professional managers" and keep the family out!" More and more, families and consultants recognize that when objective strategies are put into place, families can work harmoniously together to run profitable businesses. Thoughtful guidelines for entry, developed in consultation with a number of family members, can foster such conditions.

25

PREPARING SUCCESSORS

Once the decision to join the family business is made, how are youngsters prepared for leadership? The following chapter gives one example of how that has been done.

In Chapter 24, "Joining the Family Business," we described guidelines for family members entering the family business. Another dilemma faced by many business owners is how to prepare successors so they will be successful. The following story illustrates one such dilemma and how it was resolved.

Don Callahan came to my office with a concern. His oldest son Jay had left their printing business last year in the midst of great frustration and turmoil. After eight years in the business, he wanted more power and control, but Don didn't feel he had the ability yet. Jay's departure was a big loss for Don, as he had always envisioned that Jay would be his successor.

Now Steve, his youngest son, was about to graduate from college. Although Steve had never before seemed interested in joining the business, he told his dad he would like to give it a shot. Don said he wanted to develop a training program so that Steve would "learn the business right" and wouldn't suffer the same problems he and Jay had experienced.

After some discussion, I gave Don a fairly standard piece of advice (particularly relevant for this family). "Have Steve work for another printer first. Let him gain some experience and confidence working for someone else before he comes to work for you. That way he'll know that his accomplishments are his own — and not because he's the boss's son — and that the criticism he receives is fair and objective — not just because he's your son." I also explained that Dad will seem smarter when he sees other printers' operations. Additionally, if he works for a larger printer, he may bring back some good ideas.

Don was worried that if Steve went to work for another printer before he came to work for the family business, he might not come back: a risk he was not willing to take. Somehow he didn't trust that future ownership, direct line to management and the joys of working with family would be enough to entice Steve "if he got away." The disappointment lingering from Jay's departure appeared to cloud Don's ability to look at Steve's situation more objectively.

So we went to work designing an apprenticeship program to offer Steve the opportunity to learn the business from the inside. Don made the assumption that Steve would want to run the business eventually. "Who wouldn't!" he exclaimed.

Our next step was to sit down with Steve to discuss his goals, career hopes and plans, as well as his concerns about joining the business. With some reservations (e.g., concerns whether he would have to work 60-70 hour weeks all his life) Steve was interested in considering the opportunity to eventually run the business.

With this understanding we began to identify what Steve would need to know in order to one day take over the reins of the business and the best approach to organize the lessons. A more lengthy process was next: what does one need to learn in order to run a successful multi-color printing operation. In order to identify the knowledge, skills and work habits that needed to be in Steve's "curriculum," Dan and I helped Steve develop a series of questions to which he would seek answers from other printers, professional associations and books. After he conducted this research, we compared his observations with the work his father did. The final result: lists of tasks it takes to run the business, skills and knowledge to successfully complete the tasks and characteristics (work habits, disposition, personality traits) which accomplished people in this field seem to manifest.

Don saw many positive results from this initial process. First, Steve and he both became clear about each other's hopes and expectations which helped them start off on the right foot. Second, Steve's research gave him a deep appreciation for his father's accomplishments as well as a picture of the road ahead of him if he was to "fill his father's shoes." He entered the business with a clear picture of the time and challenges involved in mastering the business. Third, the clear delineation of tasks, knowledge, skills and attitudes helped us to craft a training program for Steve which included carefully structured positions with clear milestones of progress, criteria for length of stay in each position and appropriate supervisors who could provide training and objective feedback. Finally, Steve was excited about the program we developed, since he was involved in its creation.

The last step in this process is evaluation. The three of us agreed that periodically we would review the effectiveness of the program as well as Steve's progress. The next step would be to develop a succession plan delineating the responsibilities Don would turn over to Steve and a timetable for this to be accomplished.

The smoothest transitions between generations occur when both generations can objectively discuss the needs of the business and the developmental needs of the successor. This process enables the older generation to transmit expectations and concerns, while the younger generation can gain a perspective on what is needed to effectively run the business. This also enables them to take the parent-child dynamics out of the transition (to some degree) and focus on the preservation of the business. A timetable gives both parties a road map by which they can set appropriate expectations for the transition. Allocating the time for this thoughtful process pays off in reduced stress, conflict and pain.

26

FAMILY COUNCILS: AN IMPORTANT TOOL FOR FAMILY BUSINESS

As mentioned in the previous chapter, it is advantageous for families to develop policies on issues such as family employment. This represents one of the typical issues faced by family businesses. Another is compensation and use of family assets. The reason for these issues is the overlap of two systems: the family and the business. The gray area where the two systems overlap is like "No Man's Land" and people don't know which rules operate: family or business.

It is imperative that a forum exist for discussing these issues. It is not just an ownership issue (which could be discussed at the board of directors), nor is it simply a management issue (which could be discussed at the management team meeting). So where do family issues get discussed? Often, if no other place exists, it degenerates to the courtroom. Thus I strongly advise that families establish a family council or forum to provide a container for these discussions. The "how to's" are included in this chapter.

Family businesses are inherently challenging because they represent two types of organizational systems: a family system and a business system. Each sub-system of the family business has its own purpose, rules and expectations of members and culture. Often, we recommend that family businesses "separate the circles." In other words, address the needs of each system separately, don't operate like a parent at work and don't try to operate the business like a family.

Legitimizing Organizations

Each constituency in the family business system (i.e., owners, family members and employees) needs to have a place where its voice is heard in a legitimate fashion. When that opportunity does not exist, there is the potential for frustration and indirect or litigious actions in order "to be heard." Employees (and in particular management) have the executive or management team as their vehicle, while owners have the board of directors whose fiduciary responsibility is to be the voice of shareholders. However, in many cases there are stakeholders who are neither employed by nor owners of the family business, and they are impacted by the business (and can impact the business) in significant ways. These family members are often served well through a family council. As you will see, all members of the family — and the business — can benefit from the existence of an open forum for discussion and learning.

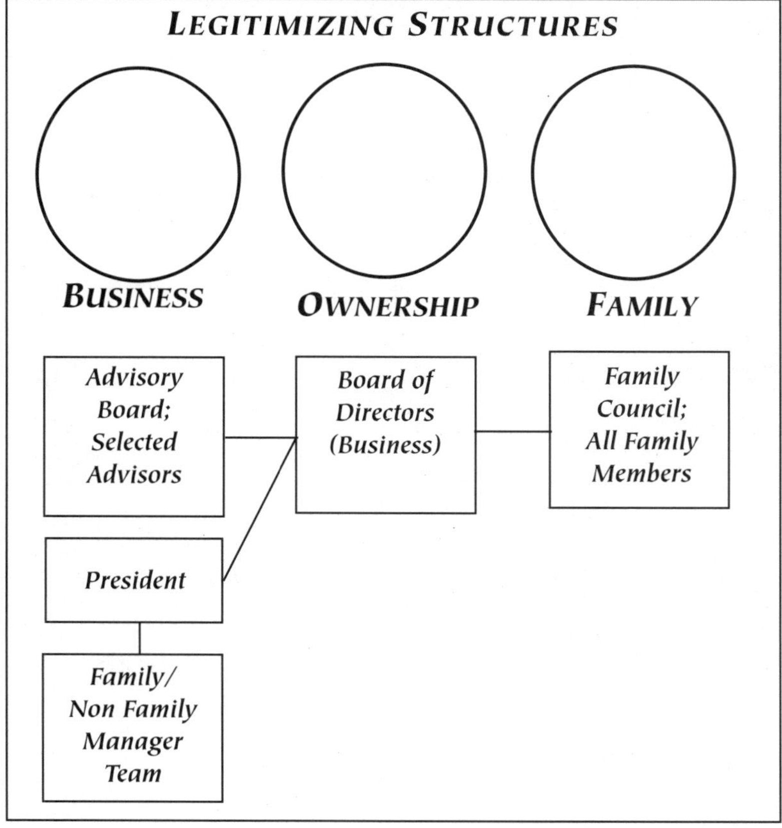

Purpose of Family Councils

Family councils serve first as a legitimate forum for a dialogue concerning the interests of the family in family businesses. Often, family members who are not active in the business get bits and pieces of information about the business. They may not get an overall view of what the business is doing, how it is performing as an asset (for family members who have an ownership position) or where it is going in the future. On one hand, family members may be tired of hearing about the business ("That's all they ever talk about!"), but on the other hand, they may feel left out of the action when they don't know what it is. The family council gives all members of the family a place to discuss the business of the business as well as the business of the family, and to deal with the interface between family and business.

Further, the family council can provide an opportunity for all family members to become further educated. This education includes knowledge about their business and assets, along with knowledge about investments, the industry or industries in which they operate, communication skills, teamwork, philanthropy and evaluation of the performance of their assets. Some families also use the council as an opportunity to support career education for its members as well as to learn about wealth management and how to cope with a range of issues related to having wealth.

Finally, the council serves as an important forum for raising and addressing issues concerning the interface of the family and the business. Issues such as family employment, access to business "perks" and assets (e.g., the company plane or apartment), and sharing of information can be discussed and policies established such that family members can feel that they are being treated fairly.

So the family council:

❧ Provides a vehicle to keep family members not employed in the business aware of what is going on and feeling included.

❧ Provides an opportunity for the family to look at what it wants to accomplish as a family.

❧ Provides a forum for looking at its assets, including the possibility of diversifying family assets into other investments.

❧ Can be a "private" place to resolve business/family issues and concerns.

❧ Can serve as a policy making board for such issues as family employment and compensation, values to be manifested in the business, etc.

❧ Can also be an educational forum regarding the family business as well as business in general.

❧ Can represent shareholders who are family members and provide a communication channel to management and/or the board of directors.

❧ Can formalize roles in the community through philanthropy, establishment of a foundation, etc.

❧ Finally, the council can provide an opportunity to strengthen the family no matter how their assets are invested.

For Which Family Businesses?

The family council can be of service to family businesses that have grown beyond the first stage of development when the entrepreneur is totally consumed by start-up. It is useful in large, young businesses (especially when there are family members both in the business and out); those in which the ownership is distributed across the family or families; as well as for businesses that have reached the "dynasty" or "holding company stage" when the grandchildren of the founders (children and nieces and nephews of the second generation) are in an ownership role. In fact, the family council can be useful for any family that wants to consciously think about ownership/family/business involvement issues and the future of each of the systems.

Structure

The family council should start with a mission statement so that everyone is clear why the organization has been established and who should belong. For example:

"To raise the level of general business knowledge, understanding and acumen of all family members so that they will be prepared to act responsibly, should they be faced with important decisions."

"We are committed to managing the relationship between the family and business in a constructive manner by developing an effective board of directors and a family council. The family council will provide a forum to further define our purpose and goals as a family, for our continuous education in business, to foster harmony and resolve issues, to provide direction to the board of directors about the expectations of the family owners and to establish policies on matters relating to the family and its assets. The board of directors will represent our interests, provide guidance to the business and assure that healthy boundaries are maintained between the family and the business."

"The mission of the Smith Family Council is to support the development of knowledge and teamwork within the family to enable us to become effective owners and mutually supportive family members."

Membership should be defined so that everyone is clear about the boundaries around the family council. I recommend that the family council be inclusive. This is the one place where all family members can gain a shared understanding of the business and the family's interests. Therefore I recommend that any family member over the age of thirteen or fourteen be included in the family council. This provides an important opportunity for kids to learn about the business; in fact, they often have good questions and suggestions. Children of this age can be instructed about the importance of confidentiality regarding information shared and learn about the sensitivity with which financial information should be handled.

Often there is a question about whether spouses (i.e., in-laws) should be included. I recommend that they be included as well. When spouses are excluded, a divisive position is established. We have found that the more family "stakeholders" are informed and involved, the less likely they are to take uninformed "potshots" from outside the circle. If there are sensitive financial issues (for example estate issues) which an older generation member is hesitant to discuss in front of "out-laws," a separate meeting for this topic can be held. One family organization of which I know even has a formal orientation process to the family council when new members join (by marriage or reaching age fourteen).

Leadership for the family council should preferably be provided by someone who is not the leader of the family business. This is an ideal opportunity to share power and responsibilities. It is important that accountability for the administration of the council is clear so that the organization does not flounder. Different leadership roles can be assigned, including committee chairpeople for different areas (e.g., philanthropy, policies, events, etc.;) facilitator for the meetings (to keep them on track;) logistics coordinator, etc. In families where there is a family office manager, that individual can support the council with clerical and organizational help, but it is preferable that he or she does not run the organization.

Meetings should be held in a business-like manner. There needs to be an element of formality even in the smallest family councils in order to differentiate between Sunday night dinner and an organized process. Frequency of meetings depend upon several factors. First, if the family is small and is mostly involved in the business and on the board of directors, then family council meetings might be once or twice each year in order to update the few uninvolved family members and give those involved an opportunity to specifically think about family goals, long-term interests and other "big picture" issues. This may occur as a family retreat. A second factor is the newness of the council and the length of the educational agenda.   Earlier in the life of the council, it is helpful to have them more often, so that the structure and education get well under way. Also, it takes time to "build the family team." For the newer organizations, four to eight meetings each year are within the ball park, also depending upon how much time is devoted to each meeting. One consideration is the geographic spread of the council members. If they are not located in a reasonable proximity, meetings might be limited to two to three times per year and for longer hours per meeting.

It is important to have an agenda and follow it in order to assure that the discussions stay focused, rather than slipping into family informality. The agenda can be constructed based upon the mission and goals of the organization, e.g., policies to be established.

information about the business(es) and general education: often the first meetings are facilitated by a consultant. This helps to establish a business-like atmosphere and a protocol for the family to follow thereafter. In addition, it is common to have speakers at meetings (financial advisors, legal council, philanthropists, etc.).

This is an important vehicle for education. Another important success factor: Follow up! At times, we will find that certain family members are not educated in the ways of business and do not take their roles or responsibilities seriously. If the council fails to call upon them to be accountable (e.g., by following up on tasks they have taken on), the integrity of the council is lost. It is also useful to establish ground rules for the council, meaning importance of participation, paying respectful attention during the meeting, responsibility for each member's share of the work of the council, confidentiality, etc. Finally, keeping minutes of each meeting helps to assure continuity and follow-up. This can be done simply with a standard format:

* Date.

* Members in attendance.

* Topics of discussion.

* Decisions made.

* Follow-up tasks or topics.

* Date and agenda of next meeting.

Benefits

We have found that effectively run family councils provide a wonderful forum for discussion of issues which otherwise could derail the family. Who is "entitled" to jobs in the family business? What kind of return on the investment in the family business is reasonable to expect? What values should guide the activities of the business? Is the business the best "basket" for all of our "eggs"? What direction is the business going to take in the future, and who should decide that? Is the business under good stewardship? When there is a legitimate, organized and business-like forum for discussion of issues at the intersection of family and business, we find that there is more harmony in the family and prosperity in the business.

27

OWNERSHIP EDUCATION

One issue that often arises in family businesses is: What is the role of an owner who is not active in the business, and what does that person need to know? After some research, I could not find an outline describing the education of owners. The following listing suggests the categories that owners should consider in becoming effective in that role. Family councils often take on the role of facilitating the education of family own- ers. Some of my clients have used a questionnaire form of this list to determine the curriculum needed by their own family members.

Family Ownership Education Outline

The following areas represent some initial thoughts about what conscientious owners should know in order to be good stew- ards of their assets, whether or not they are active in the manage- ment of the business:

❧ Knowledge of our businesses as an investment.

  ❧ Ability to evaluate in terms of return, financial strength.

  ❧ Market value of stock.

  ❧ Change in value of holdings each year.

  ❧ Income/share.

  ❧ Free cash flow.

  ❧ Earning trends.

❦ Debt/equity ratios, ROI, ROE, etc.

❦ Return as compared to other types of investments.

❦ Diversity of the overall portfolio (emerging as well as mature businesses).

❦ Knowledge of the business and industry(ies).

❦ Management effectiveness, trust in Company leadership.

❦ Strategic direction and position in industry(ies).

❦ Stability and strength of the Company.

❦ Awareness of the relevant industry trends, returns, challenges and opportunities.

❦ Personal planning.

❦ Personal strategic planning.

❦ Financial planning (including estate planning).

❦ Capability of evaluating investment opportunities against own plans (amount of risk, exploring returns, etc.).

❦ Role of ownership.

❦ Boundaries between ownership and management.

❦ Role and operations of Board of Directors.

❦ Evaluating management effectiveness.

❦ Effective team participation and leadership.

❦ Dealing with the psychological aspects of wealth (embarrassment, shame, isolation, educating children, dealing with "predators" and identifying trusted advisors).

28

PREVENTING FAMILY BUSINESS HORROR STORIES

I end this portion of the book with a chapter based on my latest articles. These discuss facilitating communication, as well as preventing serious problems that can occur in the family business.

For many years, we have witnessed through the media the sad, sometimes dramatic stories of family businesses whose strife or greed has torn apart families and businesses. These stories seem to lend support to the theory that family businesses can only be successful if you remove the family from the business! In this chapter, based upon a talk I gave at a Young Presidents Organization gathering, we review some of the more infamous family businesses and discuss how to prevent their horror stories.

Witnessing the Heartbreaks:
Hafts, Leonards and Binghams

The Haft family of Washington, D.C. gained fame several years ago as Herbert Haft battled first his eldest son and soon thereafter his wife in a control battle over the Dart Companies and the Crown Bookstore chain. The family's assets also included huge real estate holdings, auto parts stores, a grocery chain and a discount beverage outlet, all contributing to over $1 billion in annual sales. The battle apparently began when father, Herbert, saw an article in the *Wall Street Journal* about his son (and heir apparent)

Robert's plans in the business. He became incensed with his son's assertiveness and threw him out of the businesses. When his wife, Gloria, tried to defend their son and add some reason to the situation, he kicked her off the board and denied her access to the business she had helped to build. Herbert then installed his younger son, Ronald (who had no operational experience), as president of the business and then disenfranchised his daughter, Linda, who worked in the business as well. Soon, the couple were involved in a very nasty divorce and law suits erupted between parents and kids, spouses and siblings. The battles continue at press time, after seven years.

The Leonard Family also achieved fame in good times and bad. Tom Peters, author of *In Search of Excellence*[1] and other management books, considered Stew Leonard to be a hero whom he heralded in books and tapes. Leonard's marketing expertise helped build a small dairy farm into a farm store grossing more per square foot than any other retail operation in the world. Ronald Reagan gave him a Presidential Award for Entrepreneurial Achievement.

Stew Leonard was proud of his family business. His wife, kids, cousins, brothers-in-law and other extended family members worked in the business. But when I asked him at a conference how he handled conflict with so many family members in the business, he replied, "We don't have any conflict." That suggested something suspicious to me, since it is impossible to be in a family business without conflict. In fact, Leonard didn't believe in conflict — no one could disagree with him. Not one family member dared to raise a question about Stew's business practices, which became a problem as he established a system to defraud the U.S. Government out of millions of dollars in the largest computer-aided tax scheme in U.S. history. It's hard enough to blow the whistle at

135

---

1. Peters, Thomas J., and Robert H. Waterman, Jr. *In Search of Excellence: Lessons from America's Best-Run Companies*. New York: Harper and Row. 1982.

work — but when your blowing the whistle on your father, husband or child, it is doubly difficult.

The family patriarch is now in jail after admitting that he had skimmed $17 million over ten years from the store. He is serving 52 months in prison, with fines of $16 million in unpaid taxes, interest and penalties. Another sad story of a family business.

Many of you may recall the Binghams of Louisville, who were interviewed some years back on the television show *60 Minutes*. They were considered the first family of Louisville and owned the *Louisville Courier* along with other media properties including papers, radio and TV stations.

Their very proper existence was marred by the untimely death of the heir apparent and a second son, then dissatisfaction with the successors performance, throwing the women off the board (mother and sisters) and a lawsuit by Sallie Bingham resulting in the sale of the business and severing of most of the family relationships. This family did not communicate in person, but through letters to the editor, memos posted on the bulletin board of the newspaper, in books or in courtrooms.

The More Typical Challenges

In my practice, I have observed hundreds of family businesses, perhaps less public or dramatic, who struggle to maintain harmony in the family and prosperity in the business. The issues include:

- Succession of ownership and management dilemmas (fairness, competence, tax dynamics).

- Dysfunctional behavior (jealousy, greed and entitlement, addiction, destructive conflict).

- Unrealistic expectations based on naivete ("I ought to get a salary from the company. After all, my sister does, and she doesn't work very hard.").

In one family business, for example, the son-in-law had trouble finding a suitable job. His father-in-law offered him a job and found that he was lazy, dishonest and a thief. He couldn't bring himself to tell his daughter and she thus believed her husband when he blamed her father for all their financial and job security troubles. The business started to unravel, Brother re-entered the business, turned it around and then faced the wrath of his sister who felt she was not getting enough return on her share of this business. .

Another father dreamed of having his four sons in the business. But his way of relating was to have a "special deal" with each one and to set the boys in competition with each other. That backfired as the "boys" vied for Father's attention at each other's expense. Two left under very difficult circumstances and the other two eventually came to good teamwork with extensive outside intervention.

Then there were the sixty-year-old twins who didn't have to communicate much since they intuitively understood each other. That is, until each of their kids came into the business and had different expectations. When the conflict arose and they had no way of working it through, they tried unsuccessfully to avoid it. Eventually the volcano erupted and the only solution was a buy-out of one half of the family by the other.

And the son who always wanted to be close to his family so when he started a high-tech company he brought his retiring parents into the business without clear roles or authority and confused his wife (who already worked there) and his other managers and employees. Mom and Dad didn't understand where their roles as parents (and at times investors) ended and their roles as employees began.

An Ounce of Prevention...

In order to prevent the kinds of problems we have discussed, I would like to share three important principles:

- Always keep in mind that the family business is a complex system composed of two sub-systems and address the needs of the system. The family business system requires its own unique structure, with attention to three sometimes different groups of stakeholder and the need to invest in a range of relationships.

- Maintain the long term perspective with this system and consider how to develop capacity (in addition to using capacity) in order to prepare for the future.

- Pay close attention to the individual needs, perspectives and life stages of each of the stakeholders, to support appropriate roles, development and healthy connections to the family business system.

Now, let's discuss each of them in more depth:

- Awareness of the family business as a complex system, requiring its own unique structure, with attention to three sometimes different groups of stakeholders.

The complex family business system is composed of two sub-systems, the family and the business, each of which has its own purpose, set of rules or norms, values and history. When they are overlapping, as in the family business system, there is confusion over which norms are operative. Am I automatically entitled to get a job in the family business because I am a member of the family? Is communication at home focused on what is happening in the business to the exclusion of other topics?

Further, there are three roles one might play in the system adding to the complexity and confusion and often to conflict. One can be a member of the family, work at the business, and/or be an owner. In each role, there are different expectations, viewpoints and relationships. These roles can be in conflict with each other, causing problems within an individual (how to fire a family member) or between roles (the brother who is an owner but doesn't work in the business wants more liquidity, while the sister in the business wants to reinvest in new equipment).

Probably the single most important concept to prevent problems is to establish clear boundaries between roles in family and business: run the business professionally and take care of family goals and roles in the family.

For example, entrepreneurs usually spend the bulk of their time developing the business, during which time they neglect their families. Later in life, they begin to seek the closeness in the family and try to use the business to parent — hiring the child and parenting her by working with her. However, the parent/child relationship at work is subject to the same issues as at home. Unless you have clear boundaries around expectations of work performance, you may let your child get away with behavior or performance that would not be tolerated in a non-family business or would not be acceptable from a non-family member of the family business.

If you use the business to manage or control the psychological problems of an individual or problematic relationships among family members, the problem will end up controlling the business. For example, take the case of a widow who ended up running a chain of funeral homes that employed her children. The children were unhappy there but stayed (l) out of sense of obligation to their late father and to their mother and (2) out of fear that they could never make it anywhere else. The mother kept the business (rather than selling it) because she feared she would not see the children and the family would fall apart if the business were sold. So she made a number of poor business decisions. This is also an example of a business which initially dominated the family (what we call a "business-first family") and then became a "family-first business" in which business decisions were driven by family issues.

It is not a good practice for the business to be the "employer of last resort for the family." This can occur when the boundaries are blurred. Many may have experienced the boundary blurring when it feels like the family has lost its identity except as it relates to the business. Family members don't feel valued or truly part of the family unless they work there and know what's going on. That is a business-first family.

Despite Stew Leonard's problems in some areas, there is one story about how he handled boundaries well. If you refer back to Chapter 19, "Business Families: The Challenges of Families Who Work Together," it describes Stew firing an employee (his son) after which he offers fatherly support.   Separating the "father" hat from the "manager" hat is very difficult.

Legitimizing Organizations

A second strategy to help with this complex organization is the use of what I call legitimizing organizations: to assure communication and respect for boundaries. Each organization has its own purpose, responsibilities, communication channels, etc. For example, employees of the family business have the management team as a place to discuss the future of the business, issues and roles. The board of directors has a fiduciary responsibility to represent the interests of owners. If you effectively use the board to represent owners (particularly if you have outside board members to help educate and provide objectivity), family members can learn about the responsibilities of a board or an owner and can have input into the business in an appropriate manner. Similarly, a family council can provide a place to educate the family about the business and their roles, to allow the family to have input into the direction of the business and to establish policies and practices to assure a healthy family and a healthy business.

When each of these organizations exist and operate effectively, all stakeholders have a legitimate venue for the discussion of goals and concerns. This decreases the need to seek legal recourse or display inappropriate conflict in the office, the board room or at Thanksgiving dinner.

Polices for Complex Organization

Family businesses are difficult because they are neither just a business nor just a family. It is this gray area which is most difficult for people to navigate. Policies and practices designed by the family, for the family can help with the "gray." Further, fairness is one of the biggest issues in family businesses. Policies can help to define fair practices and give the stakeholders the opportunities to consider the pros and cons of differing policies.

For example, family employment policy or compensation polices are becoming quite common in family businesses. These policies help to clarify expectations within the family and when applied consistently reduce concerns about fairness. Each family must develop its own polices. Here are some considerations:

Family Employment: Consider six issues when coming up with the policy.[1]

❧ Who is eligible to join the business?

❧ At what point are they eligible to join?

❧ With what commitment?

❧ To do what?

❧ With what assistance/supervision?

❧ Under what conditions of employment?

I strongly encourage youngsters who seek a career with the family business to work outside the family company to earn merit on their own (or not). This gives the child the opportunity to cut her teeth in a business without that overlay of emotional issues

---

1. See Chapter 24, "Joining the Family Business," for further details.

which accompanies a young adult trying to establish a separate identity from her parents. Further, she then enters the business with knowledge, experience and perspective, giving her more credibility than merely being the "boss's kid."

Compensation: There are four guidelines I suggest you consider in the compensation policy. I recommend that families pay fair market value for the job; bonuses should be based on the performance of the company and of the individual; other distributions should be based upon profitability of company and the percentage of ownership (i.e., dividends); and gifts should be gifts, not to be confused with salaries.

Communication

Another strategy to prevent horror stories in the complex systems is to communicate openly, thoroughly and regularly. Communication should occur within and between the stakeholders in the various sub-systems. This can be very challenging, as well as time consuming.

But witness the losses (emotional, social and perhaps financial) which the Binghams experienced as a result of their inability to communicate directly with one another.

Fear of conflict often squelches communication. One founder believed that "loose lips sink ships" and so he taught the next generation to keep quiet. The spouses of the G2s (or second generation members) were left totally in the dark and knew nothing about the business, their assets or the future. Neither did the third generation (G3s). As G3s got older, became employees and/or owners, and wanted more information, the lack of sharing created suspicion and distrust. Non-family employees watched the G2s age and approach retirement age and, without other information, wondered about their own futures. Would the company be sold? Would it fold with the last of the G2s? The lack of sharing of information leaves people to fear the worst. All constituencies need to understand what is happening and how it will affect them.

Vigilance!

Be vigilant about the complexities of family business and address inevitable issues quickly: avoid denial. So often clients with serious problems saw the inklings earlier on and thought: "He'll outgrow it," or "It will get better with time." Or perhaps they felt they didn't know how to deal with it. Typically, the problem would have been easier to resolve earlier on. Miscommunication and misunderstandings breed when these problems are not cleared up promptly.

Another route to preparing yourself to deal with the normal developmental challenges of family businesses is to find elder leaders of families in business who have gone down this road (the more generations the better) and use him or her as a mentor. Or use a Young Presidents' Organization forum or other peer group of business owners to explore experience. Often you will find some new perspective to help you deal with the dilemmas faced by family businesses.

You must take a long term view with this system and consider how to develop capacity (in addition to using capacity), preparing for the future.

I find that many family business owners fail to think about the meaning or long term impact of their behavior for the family. For example, when they come home and complain about employees, customers and bankers, kids sometimes get the impression that the business is a headache not worth considering in their future. Yet it is natural to come home and ventilate. It is important to consciously expose the family to the perils AND pleasures of the family business and the other lessons which will prepare them for constructive attitudes and behaviors as owners or leaders of the family enterprise.

Educate youngsters and other family members early about the pleasures and responsibilities of assets and business. This is important if you are to avoid the three deadly sins of jealousy, greed and entitlement. For example, establish an educational process which helps youngsters learn about the responsibilities of ownership (taking care of a pet); budgeting (an allowance); decision-making (participating in choosing activities). As they progress into adolescence working in the family business, let them participate in family council activities or retreats; this will help them to learn about the realities of your business. Plan activities in which all family members can learn about your assets, the decisions that have to be made, and industry standards (take them to industry shows, have them watch relevant videos). It is useful for family advisors to participate as guest lecturers from time to time to educate the family about tax regulations and how they govern use of company assets. All of these educational opportunities help the family (particularly those not active in the business) to understand the complexities, hard work and learning that is required to effectively run the business and maintain or grow the assets. This tends to increase appreciation for the current stewards and gives other family members a realistic understanding of what they must know and to what they must commit in order to work in the family business.

Another strategy to help consider the long-range view is to articulate the family's values (e.g., a statement of philosophy) and explore with the family how to manifest these values in the business and in all other arenas of life. Consider developing a mission statement for the family. Why does your family exist? What do you want it to accomplish? This provides a framework for decisions including the role of the business in the family and the family in the business.

Next, it is usual to develop a collective vision statement for the family and the business. Where do we want to be in five to ten years? This also provides context for decisions ("we are reinvesting profits so that we can grow the company as we discussed in our vision statement"). Included in this process should be comments on the roles of family members in the plan to achieve the vision.

Finally, don't take life for granted! I remind my clients that no matter how well you take care of yourself, the beer truck could come around the corner and hit you at any time. Prepare now by educating and sharing your beliefs, your feelings and your self. I often hear people say things such as:

"The saddest thing is that Dad died before I knew how he felt about me," or "before he could tell me how he made the business successful," or "before he could tell me about good advisors."

You must pay close attention to the individual needs, perspectives and life stages of the stakeholders and to support appropriate roles, development and healthy connections to the family business system.

When the business succeeds despite the cost to the family or the individuals involved, this is not success. If the family is strong despite the cost to the business or the individuals, this is not success either. And if one or more individuals thrive despite the cost to the business or family, well, this isn't true success either. All three components must grow if the system is to succeed. Following are a few helpful strategies:

- Help kids develop their own sense of identity, purpose and occupation by (a) proudly sharing yours and (b) supporting exploration of their own.

- Prepare your own personal mission statement and encourage others to do so.

☙ Respect the different interests, challenges and changes which occur with each developmental stage. For instance, the adolescent high school graduate who may need to work at separation and might desire to be different wants nothing to do with the family business. However, the young adult may see how competitive the job market is, and may recognize the opportunity of the family business. Or, Grandfather may now spend time with family but never did when he was young and building the business.

An Ounce of Prevention and a Pound of Cure

I am optimistic. My optimism comes from watching more and more family businesses recognize the opportunities to prevent serious problems and build upon the legacies they have received to develop healthy family business systems. Fewer people now feel stigma in asking for help from friends, colleagues and professionals. When members of the family business take the leadership to promote the family business well-being by recognizing the complexities, planning ahead and comprehending the changing needs of the stakeholders involved, they offer so many people a chance for harmony and prosperity. And that leader can be anyone in the family business system.

29

COMMUNICATING IN FAMILY BUSINESSES: TALKING ABOUT THE DIFFICULT THINGS

Family councils, as noted earlier, are part of a solution to assure open and thorough communication in the family business. This chapter describes three principles that are important to keep in mind in the effort to communicate effectively in the family business.

With the intricate web of relationships in family-owned businesses, communication is particularly challenging and necessary. This chapter addresses why it is so difficult. I discuss three strategies for assuring that communication happens with greater ease and effectiveness.

Barriers to Communication

As an advisor to family businesses, members of these businesses typically share their concerns with me, and often these concerns include communication:

- ❦ "I don't want the kids to know how much we really have or they'll lose their initiative."

- ❦ "I can't talk to them about who I think the successor should be...the others will hate me. Let them read it in the will."

- ❦ "If I tell them what they want to hear, I won't have a fight on my hands. I'll give the others something too and then they won't care..."

- "I try to tell my son what I know about making the business work, but he doesn't listen: he has to do it his own way."

- "I can't tell her these things...she'll just cry and I can't stand that."

- "It's none of their business!"

- "How come I'm the last to know about things? Why doesn't any-one tell me about what's going on?"

- "I guess my dad loves me....but he's never told me."

- "My dad has never told me that he is proud of me or approves of what I am doing."

- "Mom just doesn't listen. I tried to warn her about the new, dis-counted lines competing with us...but she refused to budge."

They also describe the following challenges:

- How do we get the right people talking about the future?

- How do we discuss money, perks and ownership without hurting anyone's feelings?

- How do we handle problems with triangles in communication?

- How do we conduct a family meeting?

- How do we move from avoidance of discussion to open dialogue?

- How do we discuss problems without instigating World War III?

- When should we bring up problems such as alcohol, drugs or not doing the job right?

Many obstacles to open communication can occur in any setting and make it still more difficult in the family business:

❧ Not listening.

  ❧ Discounting what a male (or female) has to say on the subject.

  ❧ Interrupting.

  ❧ Not paying attention due to premature judging, being distracted and/or not valuing what is being said or who is saying it.

  ❧ Impatience.

❧ Anxiety, fear, or hopelessness.

  ❧ Lack of confidence that others will be receptive.

  ❧ Fear that someone will be angry or hurt.

  ❧ Feeling out of place or not welcome.

  ❧ Feeling inarticulate.

  ❧ If someone has a history of not listening, others will stop trying to communicate.

❧ Misunderstandings/Miscommunications.

  ❧ History of conflict.

  ❧ Can't seem to get on the same wavelength.

  ❧ Misinterpret what is said.

  ❧ Overreactions (strong reactions and/or taking it overly personally).

❧ Lack of direct communication.

  ❧ Speaking through others.

  ❧ Triangles.

  ❧ Innuendo or sarcasm.

Other barriers include:

* Ignorance: I don't know what I don't know, whether or not I should be involved, or what I should ask about.

* Lack of skills: How to communicate assertively and how to handle conflict.

* External barriers: Others' prejudicial attitudes, lack of extending the invitation, awareness of our interest and ability to participate and contribute, fear of loss of power or control.

Development of Family Businesses and the Impact on Communication

Further, the development of the business has an impact on communication as well. At each stage, the demands of the business effect how communication occurs and what communication is necessary. In the early stages of development of a business, communication is very informal. As the business emerges from the entrepreneur stage, the need for more formal communication within the business increases. Similarly, as we go to the next generation in the family, that informal communication pattern persists between business and family. So, Dad or Mom communicates with the family on a hit or miss basis. As the kids grow up, if there is a strong link between the family and business, the kids begin to feel excluded if there is not a more organized communication pattern.

The need for more systematic communication becomes even more intense as you get into the third generation with cousins and more in-laws. A good example of an issue concerns in-laws: Should they be included in communications? Should they talk about business or not? Do their opinions count or not? In-laws, particularly those who do not work in the family business, often feel like "out-laws," as if they live on the fringe of the business and the family. Cousins who are owners but not active in the business can get suspicious or demanding if communication channels are not established.

So as business and family grow larger and more mature, the need increases for formal communication structures. If you want to prevent problems, think about systematic communication with all stakeholders on a consistent basis. Prevention begins with the younger generation...as soon as they can communicate!

152

Structure, Safety and Skills

So how do we bridge the gap? There are three major types of strategies:

* Structure: Create the containers for communication.

* Safety: Establish a safe environment which encourages openness.

* Skills: Develop the skills and the courage to share openly and handle conflict.

Structure

One of the dangers in family businesses is to rely too long on informal communication channels. Because of the proximity of family members in the business and at home, people often take communication for granted: "I'll talk to them later." However, very quickly as businesses grow, these informal approaches are insufficient. Information overload and busy schedules create gaps in the communication. As noted above, with increased numbers of employees and family members, it is easy for messages to fail to reach their destination, and constituencies can easily be left out of the loop. Thus it is imperative that you establish channels or containers of communication. These channels can include standing meetings, regular written communication (reports, newsletters, etc.) and effective use of what I refer to as legitimizing organizations.

In assuring that communication is occurring where it should, consider all stakeholder groups: family, owners and employees.

Make sure that each group has a place where they legitimately have a voice. Employees typically have the management team as a place to learn what is going on and to raise issues. An effective board of directors represents the interests of owners (legally) and can be a place for owners to indicate their wishes. Family members, however, do not have a legitimate venue for dialogue. Thus, we recommend a family council[1].

There are several important principles for assuring that communication occurs in these venues:

- Be clear about the mission or purpose for the organization (e.g., education, collaboration as sibling partners, preserving a family connection and legacy, cultivating mutual support and fun, sharing of information and establishing policies).

- Establish norms and roles: the norm of open communication and guidelines for communicating in a constructive way. This often requires outside facilitation to get it going. Create a vision and then a plan to get there. Define roles, expectations and operating guidelines.

- Seek or create the opportunities to share in education, decision-making and handling the responsibilities. The more people who are involved and understand, the more opportunity there is to support decisions and actions.

Safety

The second strategy to assure communication in the family business is to create a safe environment for communication. One of the more prevalent barriers to open communication is fear — fear of being hurt and/or of hurting someone, fear of anger, criticism or being laughed at and fear of rejection. Creation of a safe

---

1. See Chapter 26, "Family Councils: An Important Tool for Family Businesses."

153

environment takes time, particularly if people have felt discouraged from communicating openly in the past. Openness depends upon trust: trust takes time to rebuild.

Some suggestions for fostering safety include:

* Establish ground rules: These should be your own personal ground rules that foster open communication. Examples used by many people include:

    * "Listen respectfully, and don't interrupt."

    * "Use 'I' Statements rather than 'You' Statements ("I would prefer if you wouldn't interrupt me." rather than "You always interrupt!").

* Create ground rules about confidentiality as well. Consider what confidentiality means: whether saying nothing to anyone or sharing a summary of the meeting but withholding details and quotes.

One way to think about what ground rules your group needs is to think about what keeps you from being open and see what ground rule would help address that concern. For example, if a person indicates that they feel their point of view has been ignored in the past, then consider ways of recognizing each contribution. One option is to make a ground rule about paraphrasing what has been said. Another is that the group will record points of view on a flip chart.

All ground rules should be committed to by the entire group and the group has to be willing to confront individuals who do not uphold the ground rules.

* Legitimize everyone's perspective: As indicated above, one of the most common barriers to a safe environment is the feeling that one's perspective is not valued. In a safe environment, everyone feels comfortable bringing up their points of view, even when others disagree with them. Thus it is important to set a norm that everyone listens to each other, is respectful and that there is an appreciation of differences of point of view.

Certain Native Americans have a tradition of utilizing a talking stick in council meetings. Only the person holding the talking stick is allowed to speak. When that person has finished having his say, someone else may request the stick and the floor. I have found that this is a useful tradition to use in family meetings, as well.

❧ Paraphrase! That demonstrates that you understand another's point of view.[1]

❧ Recognize that a trusting environment takes time and don't discount others' hesitation or reservations but identify and address them.

❧ Constructive confrontation is an important aspect of a safe environment. When engaged in confronting a difference, consider the following guidelines:

   ❧ Stay focused on issue (pros/cons, etc.).

   ❧ Stay out of triangles: give feedback directly (e.g. behavior feedback).

   ❧ Create dialogue: share assumptions rather than conclusions.

   ❧ Paraphrase your understanding of the other person's viewpoint.

❧ Keep the big picture in mind. Why do you have a family or a business? Think about the issue or challenge in the context of your mission (as noted earlier, having articulated a mission statement is helpful for this reason).

❧ Use outside resources to help break the ice (particularly in discussing the indiscussible, see below). Sometimes establishing a new forum is awkward and someone skilled in establishing forums for communication, teaching skills and defusing conflict is useful at the start.

155

---

1. See Chapter 7, "So What You Are Saying Is: A Guide to Successful Listening."

Skills

We have discussed how to establish the structure and foster safety in the environment. The last strategy is more of an individual development or "micro" strategy. On this level, we must develop the courage and confidence to overcome the barriers:

- To ask for information (and maybe overstep your bounds).

- To share information (and risk kids losing their incentive to work).

- To share feelings (and risk hurting someone's feelings, displeasing them and losing their approval or support).

- To share observations or beliefs and stir up conflict or rejection and risk pain, loss of control or being cut-off.

It can help to learn skills in effective communication, problem solving and dialogue. These include:

- Listening skills: particularly paraphrasing.

- Evaluation of our opinion, systematically addressing options and considering all points of view respectfully.

- Assertive communication (including behavior feedback).

- Recognizing our own psychological barriers and addressing them.

The family council is a great place to share lessons or learning experiences to enhance communication skills. The training received can be immediately put to use and practiced!

Discussing the Indiscussible

I have found there are a series of topics which many people find difficult to discuss: the "indiscussible." These include:

- Money.

❧ Drugs and alcohol and/or other "shameful" behavior.

❧ Work performance problems.

❧ Interfering in-laws.

❧ Getting family members to leave the business (either "problem" employees or the founder).

157

All these topics are easier to discuss when dealt with respectfully and in context. The chart below lists appropriate contexts for such conversations.

For example, it is much easier to discuss money (e.g., how we should use it) if we have the context of shared values and goals. If we know that it is important for the family to be philanthropic and support certain causes, then it makes sense to decide to budget a certain amount on a periodic basis to that cause. If we know that certain groups are "taboo" in the family, we could agree that as a group we would not support them. But the beginning point is clarity about values.

DISCUSSING THE INDISCUSSIBLE	
Topic	*Context*
Money.	*Shared values, philosophy and goals.*
Drugs, alcohol, and other "shameful" behavior.	*Impact on individual, family, and business.*
Work Performance Problems.	*Individual esteem, requirements to keep the business healthy.*
Interfering in-laws.	*Education on family business boundaries and in the context of a family council.*
Getting family members to leave the business (either the founder, or "problem" employees).	*Vision of the family business future and requirements for continuity.*

Another example: alcohol abuse. I can discuss my concern about your abuse (in my opinion) of alcohol if I do so in the context of how it is affecting me and the business. The tangible or observable impact will be useful for you to understand.

Instead of being fearful of discussing the "indiscussible," consider an appropriate context and share from your point of view. I find that the subjects that are the most difficult to discuss are often the most important to discuss.

I have also found that most people want to have the benefit of satisfying relationships with their family. Many don't know how to establish healthy adult-adult relationships, or how to restore connections which been lost or lessened over a generation. But many people respond when someone offers to build the bridge, call the meeting or host the gathering. I hope that you will take the initiative to create the setting, to model behaviors that enhance safety and to offer opportunity to develop new skills. We often wait for someone else to do it, thinking we have unlimited time. Sadly, time passes by and opportunities can be missed forever. Take the opportunity now.

I've written a poetic reminder of why:

Remember, Before It's Too Late

I never knew that I meant that much to you
I never knew you cared what I thought
I always thought you knew everything
but chose not to share with us

You seemed so confident, yet quiet
I thought you could but wouldn't
I yearned to be close to you, to know you
and for you to love and appreciate me

I understood that our family had a code of silence
when it came to talk of feelings and relationships
I was too obedient to break that code
I feared your disapproval or scorn
so I went elsewhere

Now I have my own friends and children
and I hear your request to be close
but the distance that slowly grew up through the years
is hard to bridge

My heart aches for the lost hours and days
for the time I could have learned from you
and you from me
and the adventures we could have shared
I see how you relate to the grandchildren now
and am jealous
I wish we would have had that bond, that closeness
But you were busy then, and the drain of the business
left little energy for us

I must hold on to the realization
of how precious are these connections;
how precious and fragile
and how much investment they require

As I look back at what we missed,
I want to try to cultivate what I can
with the too few days that might be left
with you
and with my own children

I keep recalling the phrase
"There's no sadder thing,
than what might have been."

EPILOGUE: SUCCESS AND PREVENTION

In a sense, having a chapter near the end of the book on prevention is appropriate. Prevention has been a theme of my work throughout my career. Ultimately, if we can help prevent unnecessary misery and waste and instead promote effectiveness and well-being, we have achieved success. Perhaps Emerson's poem captures it best for me.

> *To laugh often and much*
> *To win the respect of intelligent people*
> *and the affection of children*
> *To earn the appreciation of honest critics*
> *and endure the betrayal of false friends;*
> *To appreciate beauty;*
> *to find the best in other;*
> *To leave the world a bit better*
> *By a healthy child, a garden patch*
> *or a redeemed social condition;*
> *To know even one life has breathed easier*
> *because you have lived.*
> *This is to have succeeded.*[1]

I hope that in some way, this book has helped you to breath easier, and perhaps to find the best in another.

---

1. Emerson, Ralph Waldo. *Success.*

Notes

Notes

Notes

<u>Notes</u>

<u>*Notes*</u>